Out of Control

Who's Watching
Our Child Protection Agencies?

by Brenda Scott

Huntington House Publishers

Huntington House Publishers
P.O. Box 53788
Lafayette, Louisiana 70505

Library of Congress Card Catalog Number 94-76353
ISBN 1-56384-069-3

Dedication

This book is dedicated
to my best friend and husband,
Jimmy.
His sense of humor,
loving support, and godly spirit
have made our lives a great
adventure.

Contents

Acknowledgment

I wish to acknowledge all those who have shared their struggles, those who are working to change the system, and the families unjustly trapped in its clutches. Special thanks is due the people of V.O.C.A.L., who unselfishly shared their resources.

Introduction

A beguiling face flashes across the television screen as the newscaster recounts with horrifying detail the tragic, brutal end of a precious life. Another child has died.

Appalled by stories of child abuse, Americans have turned to the government for solutions. But, the very institutions entrusted with the care of victimized children are often the greatest perpetrators. Granted almost unlimited authority, Child Protective Service (CPS) workers have become judge, jury, and executioner. But, unlimited power breeds unlimited abuse.

Out of Control explores the liberal agenda of CPS; the blatant abuses of the system; and the changes needed to stop this assault on the family—before all our children become wards of the state.

The Nightmare Begins

The System in Action

Eight May 1989: A dark figure crept through the window of a ground-floor naval housing apartment during the night. Quietly, the intruder snatched eight-year-old Alicia Wade from her bed and slipped back out of the window. Once safely outside, the man savagely raped and sodomized the child. Finished with his brutal attack, he returned Alicia to her bed. The dazed girl walked into her parents' room, got her kitten, and went back to sleep.

Nine May 1989: Denise Wade got up and checked on the children. She was surprised that the window by Alicia's bed was open. At 6:45 A.M. Alicia woke up and complained to her parents that it hurt to go to the bathroom. The Wades did not examine her, thinking that she was possibly getting a recurring urinary tract infection. When Alicia continued to complain, Jim and Denise drove her to the naval health clinic.

As Alicia undressed and lay down for the routine exam, her parents were horrified to see that her genital area was seriously lacerated. When questioned about what had happened, the traumatized child simply replied, "I don't know."

"'There's something wrong here,' said Ronald Hawkins, the examining doctor. 'I'll have to report this.'

'You're —— right,' said Jim, breaking down in tears. 'Someone hurt my little girl.'"[1]

Alicia was rushed to a nearby hospital for treatment. While her frantic parents waited in a separate room, the child confided to the examining doctor that a stranger had crawled through her bedroom window, kidnapped her, and hurt her. Next, she described her attacker to a policewoman as a white man with brown hair, freckles, and a pimple on his chin. She even correctly described the color of her assailant's car. During a subsequent trial, Alicia repeated this description of her attacker. Even though the victim was obviously an eyewitness to the crime, the county prosecutor objected to her testimony as hearsay evidence. Incredibly, the court sustained this objection.[2]

From the onset, the police and social service workers refused to believe the child. Social workers are trained to see claims of innocence as evidence of guilt. In a stinging rebuke, the grand jury that reviewed the case said Alicia's denial that her father had raped her was "the only response the system was looking for."[3]

The Wades were not informed of Alicia's testimony, and, for the next several hours, Jim Wade was subjected to an aggressive inquisition. Throughout the day, police accused him of the most heinous crime imaginable: raping his own daughter. One officer repeatedly stated, "Why don't you just be a man and admit it."[4]

Suspicions were further aroused when questioning revealed that Denise had been incestuously raped as a child and that Jim, a chief petty officer in the navy, was a recovering alcoholic. Based upon the social service assumption that parents are guilty unless proven otherwise and the inane "risk assessment" profiles used by these so-called professionals, Jim Wade was immediately branded a rapist. Without benefit of due process, he was found guilty.

In a desperate attempt to prove his innocence, Jim agreed to have the home searched; and, he submitted to a rape test, a DNA test, and three polygraph tests.[5] No physical evidence was found to indicate the father's guilt. The DNA test, which could have immediately exonerated Jim Wade, was not used at this time because semen samples on Alicia's nightclothes were not tested for two years.

Kidnapped Again

Terribly shaken by the horrendous ordeal she had suffered, Alicia asked to go home. Now, more than at any time in her life, she needed the loving support of her family to help her heal. But, this was not to be. The "child-savers" had determined that she would be better off with strangers.

On 11 May, the Department of Social Services (DSS) filed a dependency and neglect charge against Jim and Denise for "allowing" the rape to occur. The next day, social workers kidnapped Alicia and placed her in foster care. It would be a full year before Alicia would be allowed to see her mother, and over two years before she would see her father.

Frantic to be reunited with their hurting child, the Wades agreed to play by DSS rules. Social worker Diane Anderson referred the parents to a family counselor, Kathleen Goodfriend, of the La Mesa Village Counseling Group. Hoping to find an objective professional, the Wades met with the counselor that same day. However, on the very first visit, Kathleen Goodfriend accused the father of the assault. According to the family, this was the "start of a two and one-half year campaign to convict the father and have Alicia adopted, a campaign that included concealing evidence and inducing confessions and accusations by fraud, coercion, and perjury."[6] A San Diego grand jury concurred that "social workers had lied, falsified evidence, and disobeyed court orders, and that such actions were typical."[7]

Psychological Malpractice

In June 1989, Alicia discussed the assault with her temporary foster parent, once again insisting that her father was innocent. The foster parent relayed this information to Anderson and Goodfriend. Yet, both women ignored the evidence and quickly moved Alicia to the Gregorys, a couple interested in adopting the girl.

At this point, Kathleen Goodfriend began a brutal brainwashing campaign, paid for by federal tax dollars.

For thirteen months, Goodfriend met with Alicia twice a week. According to court documents filed by the family, this "counselor" repeatedly told the child:

> (1) she knew Alicia's father had molested her; (2) Alicia would feel a lot better if she admitted it; (3) the "story" Alicia had been telling was not believable; (4) Alicia's mother had been assaulted by Alicia's grandfather [this information was imparted without Denise Wade's consent]; and (5) *if she wanted to go home, Alicia would have to say her father was the perpetrator* [Emphasis added]. At Goodfriend's direction, Mrs. Gregory also took Alicia to the bedroom "every night" and said "over and over again" Alicia's father had raped her. *Mrs. Gregory kept telling Alicia she would have to say her father was the perpetrator if she wanted to go home* [Emphasis added].[8]

A grand jury later discovered that the therapist had also used her position to teach the eight-year-old about masturbation "without any parental input or any apparent interest by the child."[9]

During this entire time, Alicia remained completely cut off from her family, even though the court had ordered visitation in October 1989. But, as is often the case, the child-savers refused to obey court orders.

In the spring of 1990, a juvenile court judge expressed an interest in talking to Alicia in chambers. The police wanted Alicia to participate in a line-up to identify a possible rape suspect, and a deposition hearing was scheduled. In a complaint filed by the family, they contend that Goodfriend and the Gregorys feared "the judge would hear Alicia's desperate pleas to go home and so stepped up their efforts to get Alicia to accuse her father."[10]

The family's suit contends:

> Goodfriend's May 1990 notes say "I'm really starting to put the pressure on now," and "she's almost ready to tell." Under intense pressure from Goodfriend and the Gregorys to change her story; and reminded that this was the only way she could

go home, Alicia yielded at the end of June 1990, finally telling the Gregorys that her father was guilty, and the Gregorys in turn "reported" it. Coached by Goodfriend and Mrs. Gregory, Alicia testified against her father in July.[11]

But, Alicia had been lied to. Neither the counselor nor the family seeking to adopt her ever intended to let her return home. With the help of social services, Alicia's coerced testimony—which violated rules of evidence and professional ethics—was used to keep her ensnared in the system.

In September 1990, Denise Wade and Joshua, Alicia's younger brother, were ordered to begin "conjoint" therapy with Alicia. Using this platform, Goodfriend unleashed her venom against the entire family. According to court documents,

> Goodfriend (1) ordered the mother to treat the father as if he were "dead" when Alicia was present; (2) accused the mother in front of her young son Joshua of participating in Alicia's rape; and (3) informed Alicia without first obtaining the mother's consent that Alicia's mother had been raped by Alicia's grandfather.[12]

After two months of brutal abuse at the hands of this "therapist," Denise Wade could no longer cope. One day in November 1990, she downed a bottle of sleeping pills. "'I wanted the hurting to stop,' she says. 'I gave Jim the empty bottle and said, Bye.'"[13] Jim got her to the naval hospital, and Denise began an eight week stay in the psychiatric ward. One month after the suicide attempt, Jim Wade was arrested and charged with raping and sodomizing his little girl.

A Conspiracy to Convict

What makes this story even more tragic is that the police investigators, the social worker, and the therapist were all aware of the probable identity of Alicia's assailant within days of her attack. Yet, the events that transpired seem more fitting for a made-for-television movie than real life.

In May 1989, shortly after Alicia's abduction, a convicted child molester entered a bedroom window in an apartment across the street from the Wades', abducted a four-year-old girl, and attempted to rape her. In July 1989, Albert Raymond Carder was arrested and charged with kidnapping and raping a number of young girls, all in Alicia's neighborhood. DNA tests were run on the semen traces from all of the victims except Alicia, and the other girls were allowed to view Carder in a line-up. Twenty-six-year-old Carder, a pedophile with brown hair and freckles, was convicted of four counts of rape and sentenced to seventeen years in prison.

After Carder's arrest, Jane Via, the deputy district attorney prosecuting the case, contacted Goodfriend and reviewed the similarities between the charges against Carder and the assault on Alicia. Alicia's description of the perpetrator matched Carder perfectly, even to the color of his car. The footprint found outside of Alicia's window, which did not fit Jim Wade's, was the same size as Carder's. On the basis of these similarities, Via ordered the blood tests on Carder, which eventually led to his conviction.

Yet, for some incomprehensible reason, Goodfriend and Via agreed to not have Alicia view a line-up. In August 1989, Via began prosecuting Carder; yet, by apparent mutual agreement, all information regarding the similar rapes, Carder's existence, and his subsequent conviction, was kept secret from the Wades and their attorney.[14] According to complaints filed in district court, the social worker Anderson also participated in suppressing this vital evidence.

> According to the complaint, when DSS worker Anderson turned over her logs to attorney Present [court-appointed defense counsel for Jim Wade] two days before trial in July 1989, she had "whited-out" information tending to exculpate the father—i.e., references to the Carder molest and the fact that Alicia had never changed her story.[15]

To add a disturbing twist to the scenario, Jane Via left the district attorney's office after the Carder conviction and joined the county counsel. She was then given the Wade case to prosecute! In a complaint filed in court, the Wades alleged:

> In June 1990, after learning Carder had been positively identified in the rape of a four-year-old and that the detective now had reservations about Alicia's father's guilt, the DSS worker and Goodfriend discussed ways to twist the detective's statements; and in August 1991, Via perjured herself about the facts in the Carder molest cases.[16]

Fortunately for the Wade family, naval intelligence officers had been conducting a separate investigation into the allegations against Wade. In January 1990, a sympathetic officer gave Jim a file containing all of the information the navy had gathered on Albert Carder. Wade shared this information with his new attorney. Then, in April 1990, Carder was convicted of yet another rape in the same neighborhood. In this case, the child had been taken out of a window at night while her mother slept in the same room. Despite the similarities in the cases, the county proceeded with the prosecution of Jim Wade.

At the time of the rape, Jim had voluntarily undergone DNA tests to prove his innocence. However, the county prosecutor's office claimed that there were no semen samples on Alicia's clothing. In March 1991, the district attorney prosecuting the father for rape uncovered the fact that a private lab had discovered a semen stain missed by the first forensics expert. Yet, the prosecutor did not disclose this vital piece of evidence to the defense attorney. When the defense attorney finally learned of the discovery of the stains, he moved for further testing to be done and asked that the juvenile court proceedings removing Alicia from her family be reopened based upon new evidence.

If the prosecutor really believed in Wade's guilt, this would have been the perfect opportunity to get positive evidence to take to court, yet the county dragged its feet.

The test, which requires less than a month, took seven months. After DNA tests on the semen exonerated the father, the District Attorney's office required that the tests be repeated and still prohibited contact between the father and the daughter. Worse, the grand jury identified a race against time to arrange for Alicia's adoption prior to the availability of the DNA results.[17]

In August 1991, prior to getting the test results, Via joined with Goodfriend and the Gregorys, asking the court to have Alicia permanently adopted by the Gregorys. Shortly before the final hearing, the new forensics expert, Dr. Ed Blake, completed tests that proved that Alicia could *not* have been raped by her father. On 15 October 1991, the court halted the adoption proceedings. Two days later, Dr. Blake announced that Carder's blood type fell into the 9 percent of the population whose preliminary DNA matched that of Alicia's rapist.

Although innocent, the Wades were not immediately given their daughter. On 31 October, Jim Wade was able to visit Alicia for the first time in over two years, under the ever-watchful eye of a social service worker. "'She just ran up to me and jumped into my lap,' Jim says. 'I started crying.'"[18] Finally, on 15 November 1991, the court ordered all charges dropped against Jim Wade, and the family was reunited.

When Alicia finally returned home, she was using medication to which she was allergic, her glasses were missing, and there was no record of any eye exams during her long vigil. Though they were fortunate enough to have insurance that covered the court-ordered therapy and most of the psychological screening, this innocent family was financially ruined by costs exceeding $260,000— prior to being billed for the foster care!

Story Not Unique

The Wades' nightmare is not unique. A San Diego grand jury investigation discovered in that county alone over three hundred cases that contained similar abuses, and 35 to 70 percent of the foster children "should never have been removed from their parental homes."[19] In spite of the grand jury's stinging criticism of the parties involved, Via continued to prosecute cases, Anderson remained employed by Social Services, and juvenile court continued to make "lucrative referrals" to Kathleen Goodfriend. "When asked if Goodfriend's performance in the Wade case might be grounds for change, Juvenile Court Judge Federico Castro said the standard for review of therapists was 'innocent until proven guilty.'"[20] It's a shame that same standard wasn't used for Jim Wade.

By the child abuse industry's own figures, over one million people are falsely accused of child abuse each year in this country. It's time for the nightmare to end.

Chapter Two

Child Protective Services: A Brief History

There is no question that the tragedy of child abuse exists. For centuries, children were considered expendable property to be sold as slaves, sacrificed to gods, or discarded as unwanted arrivals. In Rome, it was common practice to throw unwanted babies—especially females—into the streets or on refuse dumps to die. As the Christian Church in Rome began to grow, groups of "prolife" believers would scour the city nightly rescuing these precious lives. The babies were then placed with families willing to raise them as their own.

Poor Laws

It wasn't until the seventeenth century that governments became involved in "child-protection" in any significant way. Appalled by the deplorable conditions in the slums, England created "Poor Laws." These laws allowed wealthy families to adopt poor children, ostensibly to provide them education and job opportunities they would not otherwise have.

Though well-intentioned, this impersonal government intervention did not always alleviate the suffering of poor or neglected children.[1] Placed in orphan asylums, they were often warehoused by greedy individuals who stole funds intended for provisions, hired children out for manual labor, or sold them as servants to middle and upper class families. The abuses of this system were graphically exposed in Charles Dickens' classic novel, *Oliver Twist*.

As early as 1735, the American colonies passed laws that allowed abandoned or neglected children to be "bound out" to another family in an indentured or apprenticed capacity.[2] The primary motive for this was to reduce crime committed by hungry, unsupervised youth and to give them an opportunity to learn a trade. For the most part, there was little intervention into family relationships. As cities grew, however, the local communities became more interested in the plight of children. By 1925, statutes began to appear which gave legal sanction to local authorities to intervene in cases of parental abuse or neglect affecting health, morals, or education.[3]

The Child-Savers

Charitable societies for the prevention of cruelty to children were formed in most major cities. With the enthusiasm of crusaders, these organizations referred to themselves as the "child-savers." By 1933, New York City law stated that city officials could commit abandoned, suffering, neglected children, or children with "immoral" mothers to poorhouses or indentures.[4] Because these agencies were seen as helping the poor, it was assumed that they always worked in the best interests of the clients—an assumption that still exists today. As a result,

> there have been few controls over them to make them publicly accountable for meeting this mandate. Often these agencies have taken the role of parent as well as benefactor. Rarely has their intrusive power over their clients' lives been challenged or their policies exposed as coercion masked as paternalistic benevolence.[5]

Obviously, these societies did rescue some children from horrendous situations. But, the child-savers were given almost unlimited power with little or no accountability, a situation that invariably leads to abuse. No standards existed, and decisions to remove children were up to the arbitrary whims of the individual agents. Reports from these agencies show that such decisions were often influenced by prejudices regarding religion, national origin, or economic status.

One such organization was the Children's Aid Society of New York, whose mission was to clear the streets of

New York City of poor and neglected children. It theorized that if children could be removed from their parents' influence and placed in institutions or other alternate surroundings, they could be saved from an inevitable life of crime.[6]

To accomplish this end, hundreds of children were sent West on orphan trains to be adopted by farmers, shopkeepers, and other families. For some of these children, the new environment was a vast improvement, but not all of those shipped West were orphans. Many had loving parents whose only crime was poverty. For these families, this was the epitome of cruelty.

Mary Ellen (1874)

Mary Ellen was a young child allegedly abandoned by her mother after her father was killed in the Civil War. The Department of Charities placed the eighteen-month-old with foster parents under a contract of indenture that required that she work for them until she was eighteen. Here the unfortunate girl was subjected to regular beatings.[7] Finally, a dying neighbor reported the abuse to a Mrs. Wheeler of St. Luke's Methodist Mission. Mrs. Wheeler appealed for help. Since the child was not with her birth parent and had been placed in this foster home by a child-saver organization, most agencies were reluctant to interfere.

Mrs. Wheeler eventually persuaded the Society for the Prevention of Cruelty of Animals to launch an investigation and petition the court to remove the little girl from the home. When the agency went to the foster home, they found Mary Ellen covered with bruises and suffering from a cut near the eye caused by scissors. The child later testified against her foster parents, and the foster mother was sentenced to one year in prison for assault. Then the courts, in their great wisdom, placed this eight-year-old abuse victim in the "Sheltering Arms" asylum for delinquents! Mary Ellen remained in this inappropriate setting until Mrs. Wheeler appealed to the judge and offered to adopt the child.

During the trial against the foster parents, "it was revealed that the Department of Charities had several hundred children similarly placed, but the department social workers never checked to see how the children were faring."[8] The indenture contracts only required that the foster parents report on their ward once a year. No one ever followed up to see if their reports were accurate or if the child had been placed in a setting much worse than the original home.

The case of Mary Ellen was notorious in its day and should have brought a cry for reform and accountability of the child-savers and foster care system. Instead, it became the cry for even more powerful child protective agencies. One direct result of this case was the organization of the New York Society for the Prevention of Cruelty to Children (NYSPCC) in December 1874. This organization was given almost unlimited power "to seek out and rescue from the dens and slums of the City the little unfortunates whose lives were rendered miserable by the system of cruelty and abuse which was constantly practiced upon them by the human brutes who happened to possess the custody or control of them."[9]

The NYSPCC was given power under laws passed in 1875 to bring complaints regarding child abuse to court, to place children into temporary custody whenever they deemed fit, to conduct investigations into child abuse, or to remove children who were found "in a state of destitution."[10] Then, as now, these child-savers were not trained in police investigative techniques, yet the police were instructed to assist them in carrying out their duties. Originally, the agencies sought out abandoned children. Now, they were empowered to move into the homes.

Growth of a Monster

As their power grew, these child-savers became increasingly more defiant to outside supervision. In most states, they were no longer considered charities, but operated as law enforcement agencies. In fact, statutes were passed actually granting police powers to these agents. At one point, the NYSPCC challenged the court's authority to return a child to its home without the society's consent.[11]

It is important to remember that changes were needed. Children do need to be protected from abuse. Yet, this authority should have been given to trained police officers, not untrained social workers on a mission. Police are taught objective, investigative techniques—a very necessary ingredient if the presumption of innocence and other elements of due process are to be maintained.

Given this unlimited power and scope of authority, the child protection agencies received much criticism. "Many parents feared their arbitrary authority, which seemed to be exercised against the poor and immigrants."[12] This bias was reflected in a preference for placing children in institutions over letting them return home, even when the conditions that caused their removal had been changed. Parents often referred to child-savers as "the Cruelty," and the child-savers viewed parents as the problem. Because parents were often hostile over the loss of their children, these organizations were reluctant to return children to homes they viewed as inadequate.[13] Unfortunately, such conditions have not changed.

Uncle Sam Joins In

The federal government became involved in abuse issues with the formation of the Children's Bureau in 1912. It urged the states to make child protective agencies part of the state government. The Social Security Act of 1935 included funding to state and county child welfare services, but not private agencies. With the promise of federal money, the states and counties quickly complied with the government's wishes.

The 1960s saw a renewed interest in child abuse issues. California passed the first mandated reporting law requiring physicians to report suspected child abuse to authorities. Within five years, every other state had passed similar laws. It was hoped that this would encourage physicians reluctant to betray a patient/doctor relationship to seek help for children trapped in abusive settings. At first, reports were made to police for investigation, but later legislation redirected reporting to child protection agencies. Gradually, the lists of mandated reporters grew, as did the description of what constituted abuse.[14]

Another financial incentive encouraging counties to establish CPS agencies was passed in 1962. Laws governing Aid to Families with Dependent Children (AFDC) were changed, allowing the AFDC check to follow the child. In other words, if a county removed a child receiving AFDC from his home, then the county became the recipient of that AFDC check.

The Mondale Act

In 1973, Senator (and later Vice-President) Walter Mondale held emotionally charged hearings on the issues of child abuse. These hearings resulted in new laws and regulations under the Federal Child Abuse Prevention and Treatment Act that required mandated reporting laws and separate community services for child protection. Title XX of the Social Security Act mandated protective services. Once again, money talked, and, by 1978, all states had such services. Millions of dollars were made available for counties who

1. established mandatory reporting laws,

2. provided a legal process for the "guaranteed prosecution" of child abusers,

3. provided foster and state institutional care for abused or at-risk children.[15]

Although testimony was given in these hearings exposing the woeful inadequacies and abuses of the Child Protective Service (CPS), the new regulations only made these agencies stronger. Now, mandated reporters must report even the merest suspicion of child abuse or face criminal and malpractice charges. If a social worker believes that a doctor should have suspected something, charges could be filed. In addition, every American citizen was granted immunity from all civil and criminal actions for reporting abuse—even if it is done maliciously. This stacked deck has literally drawn millions into the CPS web unnecessarily.

The traditional CPS bias against the family was reflected in the funding of this act. Uncapped funds were available for out-of-home placement and "guaranteed prosecution," while very little funding has ever been provided for in-home services. No funds were made available for defense against prosecution of false or unfounded charges. Later, in an effort to bring some balance to the system, the Adoption Assistance Child Welfare Act (Public Law 96-272) was passed. Its goals were threefold: to prevent foster care placement, to encourage reunification of families in the foster care system, and to provide permanent adoptive families for children who cannot go back home. A major requirement for continued funding was that the state make "reasonable efforts" to keep the family together.

However, the Department of Health and Human Services does not monitor the states to see if "reasonable effort" guidelines have been followed. In most instances, social workers are merely required to state that such efforts have been made—they are rarely required to show evidence to support their claims. Once an assertion that "reasonable efforts" were expended to prevent foster care has been made, the funding can be put into foster care in the form of "voluntary" placements.

President Reagan said, "You cannot have a strong, healthy nation without the family at its very base."[16] Child Protective Services, with its almost unlimited police powers, is following an agenda that will destroy that foundation.

Chapter Three

The Numbers Game

According to the American Humane Society, an estimated 2,936,000 children were reported to social service/child protection services in 1993. Forty-five out of every one thousand children in the United States were turned into the system, they claim, representing a 132 percent increase over the last decade. Approximately 1,261 died as a result of abuse or neglect.[1]

Child Protection Agencies, assisted by the media, proclaim these shocking figures as proof that an epidemic of child abuse has swept the nation. This is usually accompanied with pleas for more money and even more unchecked power for CPS workers. But, just what do the numbers really mean?

First, it is important to note that these are estimates based upon voluntary surveys of forty states conducted by the National Committee for the Prevention of Child Abuse (NCPCA).[2] The accuracy of the data is very suspect. Fact sheets from the American Humane Society—based upon the NCPCA study—proclaim "that 2,936,000 children were reported to public social service/child protective services agencies throughout the U.S. in 1993."[3] But, this is not what the study indicated. The numbers were based on reports of *abuse*, not how many children were involved. There is a great deal of duplication in reporting, and one incident can account for multiple reports.

For example, a parent who spanks his child can be charged with misdemeanor child abuse, dependency and neglect, and emotional abuse—three reports for one spanking. If it is revealed that the same child has received two spankings, then this number can be doubled.

Thirty-six states, or 74 percent of those who responded, admitted keeping multiple counts of abuse reports for the same child.[4] With this incredible amount of duplication, it is difficult to have any idea how many children are actually reported for abuse. Information from the National Child Abuse and Neglect data system acknowledges the problem and asks the states to discontinue using multiple reports of abuse for single offenses in their count.[5]

What CPS doesn't publicize is that, even by their broad interpretation of abuse, at least 60 percent of all reports are "unsubstantiated."[6] A 1990 study conducted by the Department of Health and Human Services revealed that "two-thirds of these reports (which include anonymous phone calls to 'hot lines') were not substantiated."[7] Lest anyone should see that number and doubt the hysterical rhetoric from the child-savers, the public is urged *not* to consider "groundless" reports as *false*. Rather, they say, consider all reports as having some basis in fact—the social workers simply couldn't find evidence to make the charges stick.

Workers in the field will admit that reporting child abuse is the weapon of choice in disputes between neighbors, landlords and tenants, and spouses. Montana, which had a 29 percent increase in reports of abuse, credited this rise to "the recent practice of lawyers advising clients to allege abuse during custody battles."[8]

After eliminating the unsubstantiated reports (using the 60 percent figure), an estimated 1,174,400 "substantiated" or "indicated" reports remain. How many children were actually involved, and how many duplicated reports this includes, is unknown. In spite of popular perceptions, not all of the "perpetrators" were parents. Statistics from at least 90 percent of the states included complaints of child maltreatment by foster parents, day care providers, residential/institutional caregivers, or lovers. Between 60 percent and 70 percent of the states also listed complaints against school officials, out-of-home relatives, boyfriends/girlfriends, and neighbors or acquaintances. Thirty-nine percent of the states included kidnapping, assaults, and murders by strangers in child abuse statistics.[9]

The majority of "substantiated" cases involves actions that do not pose a significant threat to a child's welfare. Statistics gathered by the NCPCA indicate that these cases were categorized and distributed as follows: "27% physical abuse, 17% sexual abuse, 45% neglect, 7% emotional maltreatment and 8% other." However, they eliminated Arizona, which classified 50 percent of its reports as "other," and North Carolina, where neglect accounted for 90 percent of all reports.[10]

Only a small percentage of those "substantiated" cases of child abuse warrants removal from the home. According to Douglas Besharov, a former director of the NCPCA, about 80 percent of all substantiated cases involve excessive corporal punishment (which to many social workers means *any* spanking), minor physical neglect, educational neglect, or emotional maltreatment.[11] Under the category of neglect are "underage" children who are left alone for short periods of time, and the states do not agree about what age should be acceptable. What is considered proper in Oregon is treated as neglect in California. For instance, in Oregon, a ten-year-old may stay at home alone, but, in Maryland, a child must be thirteen. Kentucky will intervene if the child is eight or younger; California intrudes if a twelve-year-old is left for two hours or more; and Louisiana has a statutory age requirement if the child is left to supervise others. All other states, however, allow individual child protection workers to determine if they think the child is old enough.[12]

In Illinois, lack of supervision—the most frequent charge—was the basis for maltreatment charges in more than 25 percent of all reported cases. Neglect also accounts for those people who have inadequate housing, messy housekeeping, or have become homeless. Losing a job can be a double whammy—it can cost you your children. A study in New Jersey found that one-fourth of the state's foster children were taken from their parents because of homelessness. All these are included in the CPS statistics.

Once again, these particular cases involved multiple reports. For example, if someone reports a twelve-year-old girl baby-sitting two siblings in California, three reports of "substantiated" neglect are logged. Thousands of families have been torn apart because of the opinion of a caseworker after only a few minutes of evaluation. In most cases, parents are better able to determine if their child is mature enough to remain alone than a stranger. At times, some parents do leave children alone who are too young. However, while such instances may justify limited oversight, rarely does this justify removal from the home. Yet, the primary "service" in many states is removal from the home.[13]

Irene Ibarra, a Colorado deputy social services director, admitted that social workers should be less prone to removal.

> Parents are supposed to be adequate; they're not supposed to be the Father of the Year and the Mother of the Year. But it's hard to leave a child in a place where they're not with the Father and Mother of the Year.

> I think love is a greater factor than whether or not you get cornflakes and bananas for breakfast, but it's really hard sometimes for a professional to see that this child can thrive and grow and be OK even though everything isn't like your home was.[14]

Unfortunately, the majority of child protection workers do not share these views. If more of them had children of their own, perhaps their opinions would change.

Numbers of substantiated sex abuse charges are also highly suspect because of what constitutes sexual abuse in the eyes of CPS. In Arizona, children have been taken away for sexual abuse because they have accidentally seen their parents unclothed; parents have bathed a four-year-old; or because fathers were seen kissing their young daughters on the mouth.[15] Also, these charges often arise from custody or visitation disputes. That's not to say that sexual molestation does not occur in such situations. It does. But, this has also become a very effective weapon for revenge.

Richard Wexler, author of *Wounded Innocents*, estimated that for every 100 reports of abuse: "at least 58 are false; 21 are mostly poverty cases (deprivation of necessities); 6 are sexual abuse; 4 are minor physical abuse; 3 are emotional maltreatment; 3 are 'other maltreatment'; 1 is major physical abuse."[16]

Dr. Besharov concludes that recognizing how grossly child abuse numbers are misused

> would go a long way toward reducing the current hysteria about child abuse. It also would make people less likely to believe that every bruised child is an abused child. Up to now, though, most child welfare officials—in federal, state, and local agencies—have been reluctant to correct the public's misconceptions about the size of the problem, because they fear such honesty will discredit their efforts and lead to budget cuts.
>
> Child maltreatment is a serious national problem. It shouldn't be exaggerated in order to gain public and political support.[17]

Increased Reporting

There are three primary reasons for the dramatic increase in child abuse reports. The first is increased publicity. Historically, intervention almost always occurred in indigent families. While this is still the primary target, the public is aware that abuse can occur in any economic strata. The media, always searching for a headline, has jumped on inflated statistics, creating a wave of hysteria. Yet, in spite of the increased numbers of reported abuse, there is no hard scientific data to indicate that actual abuse is on the rise. Schools, parenting classes, and the media have helped to promote the CPS philosophy that every parent is a potential abuser; spanking is wrong; every bruise means abuse; and the myth that all these ills can be resolved by more money and more government control.

Teachers are fed this same dogma. CPS claims that one out of every five children will be molested before the age of eighteen. Although these numbers were based on a flawed study and have since been refuted, child protective agencies still flaunt them as gospel (see chapter 5). If this were true, however, then at least six children in every classroom either have been or will be victims of sexual abuse. Teachers, not trained as child development psychologists, are urged to spot such children and turn them into the system. As a result, public schools have become a major source of abuse reports. Lee, a child protection worker, concurred.

> Teachers are trying to deal with issues of alcoholism, abuse, etc., which they are not trained to deal with. And teachers get so busy with this, they don't teach. We get a lot of referrals from the schools. Some of them are fine, but many are inappropriate. One school social worker called me and told me how horrible the situation was in the home because she went in and the house was dirty and there was a grilled cheese sandwich on the coffee table. I said, "give me a break!"

Mandated reporting laws, established by the Federal Child Abuse Prevention and Treatment Act, have been responsible for a significant influx of calls—many of them erroneous. Teachers, day care providers, doctors, and anyone else in a position of care over children are required to report even the merest suspicion of abuse. Failure to do so could result in civil, criminal, and professional penalties. It's better to be safe than sorry. The impact of this pressure on teachers is clearly illustrated by an incident that occurred in Jefferson County, Colorado.

Jefferson High School's principal, assistant principal, and three counselors were indicted in November 1989 for allegedly knowing and not reporting that a former teacher had been accused of sexual assault against a male student. The teachers responded with such a flood of unfounded calls that the social service department set up training seminars for the principals. During the first two weeks after the indictment, school workers made 149 unfounded reports, when 15 is the average. The calls slowed down during Christmas break but began again, in earnest, when school reopened. The social service switchboard became so jammed that additional personnel had to be placed on the phones.

Reports of "suspected abuse" made by teachers during that time included a child who was having an allergic reaction to the new family cat and a teen-ager with a hickey from her boyfriend's kiss. "'I think they're just overreacting and I don't blame them—they're scared,' said the social service administrator."[18]

A third reason for the increased volume is that everyone reporting suspected abuse is granted complete immunity as long as he claims to have made the report "in good faith." Malicious intent is very difficult to prove, and the courts have universally applied this immunity to reporters. It only takes an anonymous tip to emotionally and financially destroy a family. These provisions, which bypass constitutional rights to due process, have made the charge of abuse an increasingly popular weapon of choice in everything from landlord/tenant disputes to custody battles.

No Help for the Hurting

Efforts aimed at curbing child abuse have created a mass hysteria that hurts children who are truly being abused. Most states require that every report of abuse be investigated, even if the caseworker knows that the report has come from a vindictive neighbor. The volume of calls makes it difficult to be thorough, and abused children often fall through the cracks. Foster homes are strained beyond legal capacity with children needlessly ripped from their homes, which has led to a lowering of standards. As a result, a child is ten times more likely to be abused in foster care than in his own home!

At least 50 percent of all children who died from abuse were already known to CPS. Advocates blame these problems on a lack of funds. Besharov, however, believes "the current flood of unfounded reports is a more immediate culprit."[19]

Therapy: The Cure-All

Another reason is the incredible love affair between CPS workers and "therapists." Guilty parents are often allowed to keep their children as long as they express remorse, cooperate with caseworkers, and agree to psychiatric counseling. However, innocent parents who are hostile and deny guilt are more likely to lose their children. Social workers are taught that all parents are guilty. Hostility is seen as evidence of that—so is denial, and a parent who claims he is innocent is obviously covering guilt. Susan Gabriel, whose husband was falsely accused of molesting his stepdaughter, shared this dialogue with Richard Wexler.

> CASEWORKER: We know your husband is guilty. You've got to force him into admitting it.
>
> GABRIEL: How do you know he's guilty?
>
> CASEWORKER: We know he's guilty because he says he's innocent. Guilty people always say they're innocent.
>
> GABRIEL: What do innocent people say?
>
> CASEWORKER: We're not in the business of guilt or innocence; we're in the business of putting families back together.
>
> GABRIEL: So why not do that to us?
>
> CASEWORKER: Because Clark won't admit his guilt.[20]

Dr. Seth, a psychologist who works with victims of the child-welfare bureaucracy, describes a typical report by a CPS psychiatrist appointed to "counsel" Mrs. Jackson. Jackson, who had custody of her three grandchildren, was falsely accused of "medical neglect" when one of the children was hospitalized with pneumonia. All three children were taken from the home. Her first court-appointed psychiatrist told the court that Mrs. Jackson was not guilty and that the children should be returned to her. Entered into evidence were detailed copies of medical records dating back to the birth of each child and showing regular physical exams and vaccinations.

The caseworker, however, refused to relent. Instead, Mrs. Jackson was offered a plea bargain: If she would plead guilty to neglect and go to "therapy," she could have her children back in six months. Unfortunately, at the advice of her court-appointed attorney, she agreed. As the time for reconciliation grew near, the caseworker demanded that Mrs. Jackson have a "psychological evaluation" by a different therapist of the department's choice. During the evaluation, she defended her innocence, explained how she had been treated by the caseworker, why she had agreed to the plea bargain out of desperation, and how lonely she was without the children.

The psychiatrist, who "was a child welfare bureaucrat above all else," wrote that Mrs. Jackson suffered from a "paranoid personality disorder," that she was more "intense in expressing feeling than most adults," and that she was "currently depressed." These findings, he surmised, must mean that she was indeed guilty of medical neglect. Dr. Farber explained, "This is a standard tactic among mental-health bureaucrats: to construe a mother's distress as a 'symptom' of a 'personality disorder,' rather than as a natural response to the abduction of her children."[21]

Don't Call Us

Often, the system traps those who turn to it for help. Public service announcements, nurses' training, and media blitzes describe the compassion and willingness of child protective agencies to help families. However, families that take them up on the offer find too late that seeking help is actually held against them.

Sara Jones (real names not used) is a special needs pediatric nurse. This training became invaluable when her son, Josh, was diagnosed as "special needs." Because of brain injuries received during birth, Josh is hyperactive. In addition, he is asthmatic and requires constant antibiotics to prevent recurring pneumonia. Her professional training was a godsend, making her more prepared than most for these challenges.

Sara's husband, however, did not feel up to dealing with the stresses such a situation caused. One day he simply left, cutting the family income in half and leaving all the bills behind for Sara to shoulder. He made no attempts to see his son, check on his welfare, or provide child support.

While Sara was well trained in caring for her son, she did feel the need to have time for herself occasionally. Yet, she was reluctant to leave a difficult child behind with someone who was untrained. In her training as a nurse, she had been told to encourage people in her situation to contact social services for "respite care." The department would send out a trained home health aide for occasional relief. Unfortunately, Sara requested help.

A caseworker was assigned who agreed to some respite care on one condition: that the child be reevaluated by a physician of the department's choice. Naively, she agreed, only to have her son kidnapped by the caseworker during the evaluation. In spite of extensive medical records documenting the child's condition, this doctor, in one brief examination, decided that the child was not hyperactive. He was quickly whisked away to a foster home "where his needs could be better met." The reason: the caseworker felt this trained nurse was not qualified to care for a child with special medical needs. So, he was placed with an untrained foster parent. The mother was restricted to one hour weekly supervised visits.

The child was taken off his antibiotics and the medication which helped to control his hyperactive behavior. Within three weeks, he was rushed to Children's Hospital with pneumonia, an event the mother had predicted. Sara fought the agency vigorously, which only angered the caseworker. The stress caused by the separation from his mother and the denial of medication he desperately needed began to affect Josh's behavior. As usual, the department was not willing to shoulder the blame. Instead, the caseworker concluded, his behavior must be a symptom of parental abuse. The fact that the child behaved much better in his mother's care was immaterial.

Severely traumatized by the separation, Josh began to cling to his mother during visits, wanting to be hugged and held and reassured of her love. This looked suspicious to the caseworker—perhaps symptomatic of sexual abuse. She shared these ridiculous assumptions with the mother and restricted the mother and child to one hug and kiss at the beginning and end of the visit. At a recent court hearing, the caseworker, still arrogantly refusing to allow the child to return home or be placed back on the medications recommended by the child's personal physician for his hyperactive behavior, has requested that this little seven-year-old child be committed to a mental institution.

At the time of this writing, the child has not been returned to his home, and the mother is battling in court though the legal fees have almost devastated her. This tragic story is just one more example of why social workers need to be parents. Anyone who is so insensitive to the heart-rending trauma a young child experiences when he is separated from his mother should not be allowed to play God with children's lives.

Is Money the Answer?

The strain on CPS budgets could be greatly lessened if they were to revise their antifamily "if in doubt—yank them out" philosophy. But, staggering numbers equate to greater funding. And, laws to correct the problem are difficult to pass. What politician wants to be seen as insensitive to children? Especially in election years.

Ironically, the way Child Protective Services is funded is actually part of the problem. A program created by Congress in 1962 allows AFDC (Aid to Families with Dependent Children) payments to follow the child. These payments are placed into the county social service coffers. This program also created uncapped funds for foster care, but basically nothing for in-home treatment. The majority of the cost for foster care is still paid for with federal tax dollars.

The Mondale hearings of 1973 resulted in the Child Abuse and Prevention Act, which greatly increased the financial enticements for out-of-home placements. Suddenly, millions of dollars became available, enabling counties to reinstate recently defunded programs. The law provided:

> 1. Established mandatory reporting and immunity laws, which are largely responsible for the current increase in false reports.
>
> 2. Provided funds for the "guaranteed prosecution" of child abusers. Money was made available to each District Attorney's office if they would set up a special unit for the prosecution of sexual abuse cases. There was no incentive in the investigative process to find a charge unwarranted. No prosecution; no funding.
>
> 3. Provided foster and state institutional care for abused or "at-risk" children.

These provisions, though well intended, put the accused at a disadvantage because there was no money available to help provide for defense, and there were unlimited funds for prosecution. Not only is there an imbalance in funds, but the special units created an imbalance for the prosecutors. Previously, all prosecuting attorneys had a variety of cases; now, only a select few see child molestation cases. These prosecuting attorneys have become "cause attorneys" who lack the objectivity to concede that the accused might be innocent.[22] In fact, success in such an arena is sometimes seen as a professional stepladder.

Federal funds for molestation victims have been an incredible boon for therapists such as Goodfriend, Alicia Wade's therapist, who collected high fees for thirteen months while she taught masturbation to an uninterested little girl, tortured the child into falsely accusing her father, and drove the mother to attempt suicide. All this was financed by tax dollars. Even after the truth about Goodfriend's unconscionable handling of the Wades' case was made public, the county continued to make very lucrative referrals to her.

If therapists determine that there is no abuse, they get paid for one session. However, if the claim that abuse occurred—regardless of denials by the supposed victim—then they can receive literally tens of thousands of dollars in funds through the victim's assistance and other programs. In some states, the county can receive up to forty-six thousand dollars for therapy for one charge of molestation. Counties also receive over four hundred dollars per month per child in foster care and up to one thousand dollars per month for children with special needs. Money paid to foster parents is tax-exempt and in many states is paid on a per-diem basis—factors that give little incentive for reunification. The grand jury investigation in San Diego confirmed that many foster parents there were actually warehousing children, using this tax-free money as their primary source of income.[23]

The cost of keeping families apart is high, both in human and monetary terms.

In-Home Treatment More Cost Effective

In-home, family-centered therapy has been found to be both more effective and cost efficient. There will always be a need for some quality foster care. Seriously abused children do need to be placed in a safe setting. But, comprehensive family preservation programs, such as Homebuilders, boast high success rates and lower overall costs. These programs use intense, in-home therapy for four to eight weeks in families who are about to lose their children. They help with practical issues, such as job interview skills, plumbing problems, house cleaning, etc., to persuading parents to seek help for chemical dependencies, and learning parenting skills and conflict resolution.

Occasionally, the home situation is so volatile that removal is necessary. Yet, 80 percent of the families who have utilized this program are still together one year later. In such cases, the emotional trauma the family is spared is immeasurable. In financial terms, the savings are significant. The median cost of supporting one child in family foster care for one year is $17,500. Institutional settings range from $10,000 to $100,000 or more per

child. For families where multiple siblings have been removed, the costs are staggering. Michigan's statewide
Families First program shows a cost comparison of forty-
five hundred dollars per family for preservation services,
versus the state's cost of ten thousand dollars per child
for family foster care and forty-two thousand dollars per
child for institutional care.[24]

Child abuse is a problem, but it is not an epidemic.
Current funds would go much further if they were redirected into programs that would solve problems and
preserve families. In our concern for children, we have
granted unprecedented police power to often unqualified
people, giving them total control over our nation's most
precious asset—the family. The system doesn't need more
funding; it needs to be overhauled.

Chapter Four

This Thing Called Abuse

Abuse does occur. Every year over one thousand children die of neglect or abuse, and many others are injured. Over half of those were already under the watchful eye of Child Protective Services; some were actually in foster care. It is not the intention of this book to diminish the tragedy or to ignore the pain of the victims. But, child abuse does not exist in the epidemic proportions that child-savers wish us to believe. They have used this emotional issue as a political tool to build empires, create a multibillion dollar industry and promote a liberal, antifamily agenda. Under the banner of "Save the Children," CPS agents have been given the power to destroy the home.

What Is Abuse?

Though every state has a statute that outlaws child abuse and neglect, the definitions of what constitutes such crimes are incredibly vague. In Colorado, the Department of Social Services is allowed to interfere on the behalf of any child. The following statutes are typical examples:

> Whose parent, guardian, or legal custodian has abandoned him or has subjected him to mistreatment or abuse or whose parent, guardian, or legal custodian has suffered or allowed another to mistreat or abuse the child without taking lawful means to stop such mistreatment or abuse and prevent it from recurring;

> Who lacks proper parental care through the actions or omissions of the parent, guardian, or legal custodian;

Whose environment is injurious to his welfare;

Whose parent, guardian, or legal custodian fails
or refuses to provide proper or necessary subsis-
tence, education, medical care or any other care
necessary for his health, guidance, or well-being;

Who is homeless, without proper care, or not
domiciled with his parent, guardian or legal custodian through no fault of such parent, guardian or
legal custodian;

Who has run away from home, or is otherwise
beyond the control of his parent, guardian or legal
custodian.[1]

Child abuse is defined this way:

"Abuse" or "child abuse or neglect" means an act
or omission in one of the following categories
which seriously threatens the health or welfare of
a child:

Any case in which a child exhibits evidence of skin
bruising, bleeding, malnutrition, failure to thrive,
burns, fracture of any bone, subdural hematoma,
soft tissue swelling, or death, and such condition
or death is not justifiably explained. . . .

Any case in which a child is a child in need of
services because the child's parents, legal guard-
ians, or custodians fail to take the same actions to
provide adequate food, clothing, shelter, medical
care, or supervision that a prudent parent would
take . . .

Nothing in this subsection . . . shall refer to acts
which could be construed to be a reasonable exercise of parental discipline.[2]

What ensnares the majority of families into the child
protection system is the crime of "neglect." Patrick
Murphy, a former head of the Chicago's Legal Aid
Society's Juvenile Litigation office describes the neglect
statutes as "'one of those broad nets of legislation that
catch every fish swimming through and allows the fisher-

man to pick which he wants to keep and which he wants to throw back. Social agencies proposed it, and social agencies love it.'"[3] Depending on the study, 60 to 80 percent of all reports of child abuse or neglect are simply false, even by the loose standards of the child protection industry. The majority of the remaining cases arises from "neglect." What is neglect?

In Ohio, it's when a child's "condition or environment is such as to warrant the state, in the interests of the child in assuming his guardianship." In Illinois, it's failure to provide "the proper or necessary support . . . for a child's well-being." In Mississippi, it's when a child is "without proper care, custody, supervision, or support. In South Dakota, it's when a child's environment is injurious to his welfare." Lest any South Dakota child-saver still hesitate, the legislature added that "this chapter shall be liberally construed in favor of the state."[4]

No one would argue that child abuse laws are necessary. Parents should not be allowed to abandon, injure, molest, or starve their children, nor should they knowingly permit someone else to abuse them. However, the vagueness of these laws has given social workers almost complete discretion in defining abuse and neglect. These decisions are naturally influenced by their own values and agendas. They investigate the reports, write the complaints, and make recommendations that are almost always followed by judges. "The scariest thing to me," one Colorado social worker confided, "is that what happens to a child is completely up to the individual social worker. Most of the decisions are made out in the field without any supervision. I can't remember the last time a judge did not follow my recommendations."[5]

Abuse is whatever a particular case worker decides it should be, a situation that has created incredible injustices. For example, what constitutes "mistreatment"? Failure to give a child access to television after 7:30 P.M.; being late to pick up a child from school;[6] failure to understand a child's emotional needs; placing too high an expectation on a child; too much supervision—or too

little supervision. Using corporal discipline, placing restrictions on a child's choice of friends and "emotional
maltreatment" are also reasons to remove a child from
the home under the "abuse" clause. Failure to have a
testamentary will, working too much, and not disciplining
in a consistent enough manner can be considered "passive abuse."[7]

The category of "emotional maltreatment" is so open-
ended it could include almost any family, depending on
the whims of a particular caseworker. In a survey, child
welfare workers described what they thought constituted
sufficient "emotional maltreatment" to remove a child
from his parents. The responses included such things as
requiring one child to do more chores with fewer rewards than other children in the family; forcing a child to
wear inappropriate clothing for his maturity level (forbid-
ding miniskirts or punk haircuts, perhaps); and ground-
ing a child from extracurricular activities without "sufficient reason" as defined by the individual social workers.[8]

Dr. Monty Weinstein believes that all families charged
with "emotional maltreatment" should retain custody of
their children. He states, "In some cases counseling is
indicated, but in most cases it's merely an issue of a
caseworker imposing their own definition of *good* parenting on parents who are fully capable of taking care of
their children."[9]

Children have been removed from their homes because a parent places too much emphasis on academics
or because the child's grades are too low. "Educational
neglect" has been interpreted as an open invitation to
interfere with a family over truancy or home schooling.
If a child skips school consistently it *must* be the parents'
fault; the school could not possibly bear any of the blame
for failing to keep the students interested. And, home
schooling, which will be discussed later, is seen as a "red
flag" to many social workers, a sign that a parent has
something to hide.[10]

Parents can be charged with abuse or neglect if *someone else* abuses their child—such as a neighbor, relative,

another child, or an intruder. Before being charged with rape, the Wades were cited for neglect for "allowing" an intruder to crawl through their window in the middle of the night and kidnap and rape their child! Richard Wexler reported that a St. Louis hospital actually sought legislation allowing them to file neglect complaints against parents for failing to protect their children when the child had been raped by a stranger. One major reason for this was the fear that filing complaints against accused rapists can result in lawsuits. However, they are protected by immunity when they report parents "in good faith," no matter how damaging the charges.

Other parents, such as Sarah Jackson, claim to have lost a child because it was discovered that a spouse or boyfriend was molesting the child.[11] Even though the innocent parent gets rid of the offender, the child may never be returned. This, of course, victimizes the child a second time by removing the support system that is so desperately needed in order to heal.

Children have also been ripped from their homes because of sloppy housekeeping, which is exactly what happened to Nancy Osborn. Osborn first lost custody of her three children when her ex-husband was charged with molesting her oldest child. Although Osborn was innocent, did not live with the father, and indeed was unaware of the molestation, the daughter was taken from her home and held hostage in a foster home for a year. Two years after her daughter's return, the police and social workers showed up for an unannounced "health and welfare" check as Osborn was leaving for work. "After finding dishes in the sink, a sock on the kitchen floor, unmade beds, toys on the floor, an overflowing laundry hamper and a box of papers in Osborn's bedroom, the police took the children."[12] Good grief! What working parent hasn't dashed off to work some morning without leaving the house a bit of a mess? An impromptu white-glove inspection might have caught even a social worker off guard.

In 1988, the National Committee for the Prevention of Child Abuse spent more than $2.5 million to "tell us that parents are guilty of neglect if they give their children money to go to McDonald's for breakfast too often." They also cited compliments such as "Just wait till she grows up," as an indication that the speaker may be a child molester.[13]

Lack of Supervision

A single mother decided to allow her eleven-year-old daughter to stay at home and watch TV while she ran to the store. When she returned, her daughter was gone. An irate neighbor had turned the mother in for neglect. The girl was placed in foster care for three months until her twelfth birthday, when she would suddenly become mature enough to be left home alone, a move the foster parents contended was unnecessary and cruel.

> The girl was really sweet and mature and well-behaved. It was obvious her mother had done a wonderful job with her. We felt sorry for them both; they were so lonely. We would let her call home every night, but those three months were terrible for her. We threw a birthday party for the girl and her mother to celebrate her going home. [This child was fortunate; not many are placed with such understanding foster parents.][14]

Two children, ages eight and eleven, were left alone for two and one-half hours. After an anonymous tip, a CPS caseworker knocked on the door. The children, who were taught not to open the door to strangers, refused to answer. The police were called to break in. The children were taken and kept for several weeks although there were no signs of abuse.[15]

In order to send their children to a Christian school, a couple took on a morning newspaper route. Since their oldest child was almost twelve, the parents went out on the route together while the kids slept. This teamwork allowed them to be back in time to get the kids up and ready for school. One Saturday morning, the parents returned home to find their children gone and a note that the police had taken them for "lack of supervision." Frantic, they rushed to the police station, only to be informed that no action could be taken until Monday. An anonymous tip led to a weekend of incredible trauma. The oldest child was imprisoned in juvenile hall with delinquents for two days while the younger children were placed in foster care. The following Monday, the family was reunited on the condition that one parent stay at home with the children until the oldest child turned twelve—two weeks later. Then, she would suddenly be capable of caring for her siblings.

In some states, the law dictates that a child is not mature enough to be left alone until they are twelve. However, internal procedures do give social workers the authority to determine if a child is mature enough. Presumably, a caseworker is much more capable of ascertaining this in a ten-minute interview than the parent who lives with them. Yet, the cases cited above illustrate the capricious, illogical, and damaging way that power can be used. Each of the above examples points to a *system* that is the abuser—not the parent. These children have been severely traumatized. Additionally, they fear the very law enforcement officers they are expected to trust. (It is important to note that these cases were classified as "substantiated" neglect for statistical purposes.)

To Spank or Not to Spank

Spanking is a leading cause of intervention by CPS. David Gard's story is only one example of many. David was kidnapped from school by CPS after the agency received a tip that he had been spanked by his father. A physical exam revealed no evidence of abuse, and David explained that his father had spanked him because he had walked out on the ice while it was thin. He begged to go home, but his pleas were ignored. "'They tried to brainwash me,' he says. 'They'd tell me, he didn't do it because you misbehaved, he did it because he wanted to.'"

For six lonely months, David was shut off from all family contact while his "saviors" badgered him to accuse his parents. Finally, David was allowed in court to testify, but it took the system another six months to determine that David would be better off at home.[16] The sting of the spanking faded quickly, but the scars caused by CPS run deep. While David was imprisoned in the system, he lost a year of fellowship with his family and missed two very important events: his uncle's wedding and a special family reunion. Who was the abuser?

Colorado's statutes demand that nothing in the law should be construed as license to interfere with parents engaged in a "reasonable exercise of parental discipline." Technically, a spanking with an open hand on the buttocks is legal as long as it leaves no mark. Yet, in practice, this is completely taboo in CPS circles. Most social workers see themselves as change agents, and one of their missions is to eliminate all use of corporal punishment.

Dr. Dobson, well-known Christian psychiatrist and author, served for seventeen years on the attending staff of Children's Hospital of Los Angeles. In this capacity, he was exposed to heart-rending cases of child abuse. Still, he strongly supports the necessity of some corporal punishment in a young child's life, as long as it is administered in a nonabusive manner.

> A spanking is a very worthwhile tool when used properly, and I strongly urge its periodic application to the bottoms of America's youngest generation. However, like any tool, it can be applied correctly or incorrectly. Belief in corporal punishment is certainly no excuse for taking out your frustrations and anxieties on little Johnny.[17]

A spanking should not be used as a last resort or when the parent is angry. It should be reserved for "sassiness, haughtiness, or outright disobedience. No other form of discipline is as effective as a spanking when willful defiance is involved."[18]

Corporal punishment does not include abuse; it should never harm a child or be done in front of others where his self-esteem will be shattered. Dr. Dobson recommends that the spanking should be administered in private with an appropriate object other than the hand, such as a rolled up paper or magazine, which will not hurt the child. The hand, he feels, should always be an object of reconciliation.

However, in Colorado, this is illegal. A Denver social worker confirmed that spanking with a newspaper was considered abuse and could be grounds for removal from the home. And, Colorado is not unique in its quest to eradicate the menace of corporal punishment. Pamphlets from NCPCA announce, "No child needs a spanking. . . . Even spanking older children can be dangerous. . . . Children do not need to be hit in order to learn how to behave." They suggest that talking to a child is sufficient to correct bad behavior. If the parents are angry, then they should put themselves in "time out."[19]

The NCPCA uses natural public concern over the plight of abused children to recruit support in their move to criminalize corporal punishment in schools. Classifying spanking as "violence," they claim that those who administer such punishment

> teach destructive lessons by their examples. Children learn that it's okay for adults to hurt children, that kids aren't entitled to respect for their feelings, their sense of self-worth, or their bodies. They learn that "might makes right," and that violence is how to solve problems. Regrettably two-thirds of the states still permit corporal punishment in their school.[20]

James Garbarino, another prominent "expert" in childhood development, claims "physical punishment in the home is a bad policy because even non-abusive 'corporal punishment' . . . contributes to greater violence in our society."[21] Spanking should be redefined as "an assault against a child."[22] Dr. Vincent Fontana, medical director and pediatrician in charge at the New York Foundling Hospital, and supposedly America's leading expert on child abuse, carries this idea even further. He blatantly defines all forms of spanking as abuse and makes the ridiculous claim that

I can say without question that child abuse in one form or another is taking place in the majority of our American homes today, and the alarming part about it is that it is not being recognized as child abuse. Most parents—yes, *most*—fail to draw the line between discipline and physical punishment.[23]

Corporal punishment is viewed as the source of societal ills because it "only teaches that it's okay to use violence in solving problems, it's okay for a powerful person to hurt someone who is less powerful, that hitting is okay if practiced by certain people at certain times."[24] Dr. Fontanta bases these claims upon the exaggerated assertion that "practically every child development expert alive regards corporal punishment as an unacceptable and outdated form of discipline."[25] (Many child development specialists do *not* agree with Fontana. Perhaps he should read a copy of *Dare to Discipline* by Dr. Dobson.) He further describes any parent who uses spanking in any form as "immature, unthinking or self-indulgent" or "poisoned by his own upbringing."[26] Dr. Garbarino suggests that the state step in and eradicate corporal punishment from American homes.

What makes these comments so dangerous is that, for the most part, social workers swallow them hook, line, and sinker, even though logic dictates otherwise. Before Dr. Spock came out with his hypothesis that spanking warped a child's psyche, spanking—not abuse—was considered an acceptable form of discipline. If this invariably leads to violence, then why wasn't there an outpouring of youth violence in the 1940s and 1950s? Back then no one worried about gangs, drive-by shootings, assaults on teachers, and metal detectors and armed guards in our schools. However, since our society has moved away from spanking and stricter discipline in the homes and schools, youth violence has become epidemic.

Other Symptoms of Abuse

The NCPCA and other child-welfare agencies point out several signs of abuse. These include

chronically unkempt appearance
overly neat, girl dressed overly feminine
child is too loud or talkative
shyness
low self-esteem
aggressive behavior
passive behavior
reluctance to participate in sports
fractures, burns, bruises, cuts, welts, or bite marks
sexual knowledge or acting out above child's ma-
　　turity level
pain or itching, bleeding or bruises in or around
　　genitals
constant hunger or fatigue
lack of supervision
delayed physical, emotional, or intellectual behavior
chronic lateness on the part of the parent
chronic health problems
failure to promptly repair glasses
failure to promptly meet dental needs of child
illness or death of a parent (remaining parent
　　may become physically or sexually abu-
　　sive as a result of the stress)
family keeps to itself, does not participate in
　　community
presence of a stepfather
an untidy house
pulling a child out of school to home school
depressions, apathy, or hopelessness in a parent
　　and
reports from children about occasionally sleep-
　　ing in a parent's bed

While some of these are indeed a sign of child abuse, the majority may also be indicative of other problems, but teachers, doctors, and day care workers are told that they should suspect abuse, first and foremost. They are to report children with these symptoms as possible abuse victims and let the child-savers ask the questions. How-ever, many child-savers only "believe the children" when they claim abuse has occurred.

This opinion is reinforced by the training social workers and teachers receive. During an undergraduate education course at a community college in Colorado, prospective teachers were taught that a bruise on the back is *always* the result of child abuse, but that is ridiculous. Children can scratch and bruise their backs while climbing trees, crawling under restaurant booths to retrieve color crayons, or backing into the faucet in the bathtub. Yet, abuse is always supposed to be the first suspicion, and these impressionable students, many of whom had not had children yet, were told that the presence of any mark on the back required that the family be turned over to the child-savers. Failure to do so, they were warned, could cost them their jobs and result in civil and criminal penalties.

Accidents do happen. Children fall off of bikes, trees, and fences. Kids get hit with baseballs and bitten by younger siblings. Antibiotics can cause yeast infections and pain and itching around the genitals. Bubble bath and soaps are often responsible for urinary tract infections. After a nightmare, children often run to the safety of a parent's bed. Parents generally turn to home schooling because of the failure of the public school system to provide a superior education. Early sex education has increased sexual knowledge at premature ages. Personalities differ. Many children who are not abused are shy or boisterous or suffer from low self-esteem. Some children are naturally meticulous about their appearance, while others could care less. In spite of what feminists may believe, some little girls love to dress femininely—this does not mean their daddy is molesting them. And, many adults have poor time-management skills; but that doesn't make them abusive, nor should they come under the watchful eye of social service agencies.

The "At-Risk" Trap

In an effort to "prevent" abuse, CPS is empowered to intervene in a home where it is felt a child is "at-risk" of being abused and neglected. In actuality, social workers are asked to be prognosticators. If they leave a child in the home and he is abused, then they may suffer repercussions. However, if they remove the child "in good faith," they are protected from civil and criminal charges even if the child is killed in foster care.

Making "at-risk" assessments is basically an arbitrary, unsupervised action. The word of the social worker is always taken over the word of the accused. Some departments have internal guidelines for what constitutes "at-risk," but the actual assessment is left to the individual discretion of the CPS agent. Based on the whim of one person, families can be destroyed, reputations and careers ruined, and children are devoured by the destructive monster called "child protection."

A sample risk assessment worksheet made up by Norman Polansky and associates reveal the arbitrary and prejudicial manner with which these decisions are made. The list contained ninety-nine questions. A score of 63 was considered neglectful and grounds for CPS intervention; 77 was acceptable, though some training may be warranted; 88 or above is required for the home to be considered good.

Some of these questions were incredibly subjective or impossible to ascertain in one visit. They included such things as: whether meals have courses that "go together," if the mother seems unaware of "possible" dental problems, if the home is "dilapidated," if there are dirty glasses present in the bath or bedroom, food scraps on the floor under the table, or if the "mother is tuned into child's indirect emotional signals." Other questions reflect the feminist attitudes that toys should not be based on gender; i.e., are dolls available for the boys and trucks for the girls?[27]

The risk assessment reveals the arrogant assumption that social workers, many of whom have never had a child, know what activities are best for kids. Included in the list are a number of recreational and educational activities that good parents will provide. These are swimming lessons, overnight vacation trips, television watching, visits to historical or cultural buildings, spectator sports, parades, children's movies, visits to the firehouse, and fishing. In addition, the child must possess his own books (library books do not count), color crayons, and a toy shovel.[28] A parent could be very involved with the child, but there is no provision for other activities. Also, parents distressed over the *trash* on television and in movies will have points assessed against them.

The Crime of Poverty

Child-savers have traditionally had a great prejudice against the indigent. Early agencies often tore families apart simply because they were poor. Unfortunately, this has not changed. Children are routinely removed from homes because the utilities are shut off, even though the monthly bill for foster care for one child costs at least three times as much as the average cost of utilities for a family. Families in low income neighborhoods are more likely to be turned in by vindictive neighbors. Once caught up in the system, they seldom have the financial means to defend their rights.

Polansky's risk assessment is a blatant example of this prejudice. Questions which could be influenced by lower economic status include: meals include variety and multiple courses; house is in good repair; flooring should not be worn out, splintery or torn; living room should not double as a bedroom; and no child, no matter how young, should share a bed with a parent. Windows and screens are to be repaired within one month of damage and storm sashes should be in good repair; screen doors should be hung properly; no leaky faucets or leaky roofs; mattress must be in good condition; clothes should not be hand-me-downs; the family should own adult and children's books, a working electric vacuum, camera, television, fishing equipment, and magazines. Required activities included such expensive things as movies, vacations, spectator sports, and carnivals.[29] In all, forty-one of the ninety-nine questions are related to poverty. This is sufficient to have a child removed from his home. Based upon these standards, Abraham Lincoln would have been torn from his family and thrust into the foster care system.

Profile of the Child-Savers

"Most social service workers I know genuinely have a concern for kids, and that is why they are there. But that doesn't stop their values from coming in," a social worker in a large western city commented. "And some of the caseworkers in my unit are really scary." There are people working within the child abuse industry who support the family and who hold some semblance of traditional values. But, these are rare, and often become so discouraged that they quit. Those within the system who speak out have been known to suffer retaliation from superiors, and even come under scrutiny themselves.[30]

Many social workers have chosen their career because of abuse they endured as children. While this may give them empathy for other abused children, in many cases it gives them a distorted view of family. Their own negative personal experiences predispose them to believe that all families are dysfunctional, a perception reinforced by "experts" such as Dr. Fontana. He blames the situation on parents who grew up in homes where corporal punishment of some form was practiced, and thus they are "poisoned" by their upbringing. "The family is failing," he charges; "It seems to have lost its way."[31]

To correct this situation, he lays out a plan for state intervention that is reminiscent of Nazi Germany or the former Soviet Union. The state, through social workers, should be allowed to oversee all parents, instructing them in methods approved by Dr. Fontana.

This arrogance is prominent among CPS agencies. Free from constitutional restraints and outside oversight and accountability, these people enjoy a measure of power not given to any other segment of our society. They defy court-ordered visitations, refuse to respond to grand juries, and keep families apart even when parents are found innocent of any wrong doing. "Power corrupts, and absolute power corrupts absolutely," Lord Ashton once observed. The truth of this is glaringly apparent in child protection circles.

Most CPS workers lack the primary qualification for dealing with families: a child of their own. One social worker, who does happen to be a parent, observed:

> It's my personal opinion that until you have a child you can't possibly know what you are doing. The scary part is, three-fourths of the staff [in that city] have never had children. They are either single without children, married without children, or gay without children. Those who are married and have kids are in the minority. It's really scary. They are making all of these decisions based on a lack of first-hand experience. Yet they don't think you "need to be an alcoholic to help alcoholics." But I'll tell you what, when you are taking people's kids away and you're wondering why they are hostile, you need to be a parent.

> The second I had my first child it changed how I did my case work. I thought, wait a minute. If I was falsely accused, you don't think I'd be sitting there saying, "Okay, I'll do a treatment plan." I would be hostile. And now it worries me more when parents are not hostile. Yet most caseworkers view hostility as an admission of guilt.[32]

Anne Williamson, a former foster child, describes caseworkers as "God."[33] They hold the entire future of families and children in their grips. They write and present the cases, make recommendations, and control placements. For the most part, they are the ones who determine if a child will ever return home, and this power can be wielded with a deadly vindictiveness. One social worker described an incident that occurred shortly after she started her job. Another caseworker was aggressively questioned in court over her failure to prepare the required pretrial statement. After the hearing, she told the new worker, "'That attorney humiliated the wrong person. I'm going to write up the statement, and this mother is never going to get the child back.' That's the kind of mentality some social workers have."[34]

Educational Qualifications

Considering the power wielded by social workers and the lack of personal experience that many have at child rearing, it would be logical to assume that educational requirements would be stiff. This is not the case. The percentage of child-welfare workers with master's degrees has dropped from almost half in 1958 to only 9 percent in 1985.[35] And, those degrees are not necessarily in a related field. One woman who does child sexual abuse assessments in Colorado has a master's degree in art!

A survey of forty-eight states found that four states required entry-level child protection workers to have a master's degree in social work. Twenty-two states accepted college degrees in any field, and the rest accepted high school diplomas or had no educational requirements at all.[36]

Once in the system, the training is slanted by the liberal, antifamily dogma of the so-called experts who teach that all parents are potential abusers; that the state has the authority to oversee all aspects of child rearing; that absolute values are outmoded; and that any corporal punishment is abuse. Stepfathers and boyfriends are portrayed as sexual predators who would molest a child if given the opportunity. The family is suspect, and they, as wise agents of the state, have the right to impose their beliefs on the rest of society.

Training seminars, such as one held by Dr. Mary Case, a medical examiner for St. Charles county, are filled with unfounded, stereotypical statements. For example, she said that a messy house reflected a parent's general attitude and could very well mean that they are drug users. "Boyfriends are always suspicious characters, by the way, when they are baby-sitting," she added. Other bits of misinformation she passed on were that spinal fractures *never* happen accidentally (as a physician she should know better) and that children will never have more than one bruise at a time unless they are being abused. "Three marks on that child's face, the probability that that child has been abused is almost 100 percent without knowing anything more. Just seeing three bruises on the face of a child."[37] While bruising on a child's face is cause for concern, it should never be justification for kidnapping a child without further investigation. Active kids can get banged up on their own.

Criticism of the system also comes from people who are in it. Trevor Grant, who served as director of Social Service of CWA (Child Welfare Administration), resigned in 1991 "'in disgust'" over the arbitrary manner in which the system destroys lives. Over half of all child abuse reports—over one million per year—are false. Of the remaining "substantiated" cases, Mr. Grant believes 85 percent are related to poverty, not abuse. "For the most trivial reasons families are destroyed. If the furniture is broken down or the house is messy, CWA workers will remove the child. When in doubt, the safest practice for the workers is to remove the children and then file neglect charges that never have to be proven in court."[38]

The following letter, written by a child whose family was caught up in the web of "child protection," illustrates how destructive that system can be:

> My name is P.G.P. I am writing this letter with the help of my Mama because I have trouble seeing. I am in a special class in school because of my eyes.
>
> I think that if people listen to me my sisters Sharon, age 10, and Nikcole, age 5, will come home.
>
> Child Protection will not listen to me. They say my Mama and Daddy neglected us. I don't know really what this word means. Mama says it means that my parents did not feed us, buy us clothes, did not clean our clothes, did not take us to the doctor, did not clean the house.
>
> This is not true. My parents give us things, feed us, take us to the doctor, buy us medicine, play with us, take us places, even if they don't have money to buy something they need for themselves.
>
> Our parents love us.

Our parents help us with our homework. They talk to our teachers a lot. I wish sometimes they wouldn't only because sometimes I get so sad I don't behave at school and I don't do my homework.

Our parents have always done things with us as a family. I cry sometimes. I get mad sometimes because we are not a family anymore.

Mama and Daddy try to make things better but they are sad too. We are all sad.

I pray because Mama says only God can bring our sisters home. I pray but I think God is too busy.

My sister is locked up in a mental hospital. They say she has to live there and she may never come home because she will hurt us.

I think they are crazy because Sharon never hurt us and she doesn't try to hurt us when we go visit her. They let her visit the foster parents of my little sister Nikcole and she does not hurt her.

Nikcole tells me that the foster parents want her to lie and say Sharon tried to hurt her. Nikki says she won't do it.

They also let Sharon go to a foster home on weekends with two kids in it. She doesn't hurt them.

Why do they lie about my sisters?

Why do they want to hurt my family?

Why can't we be together? [reprinted with permission]

Vague child abuse laws need to be rewritten to clearly define what constitutes abuse, thereby limiting the horrendous power now afforded to often unqualified, prejudiced individuals. In no other segment of our society are a handful of people given the power to destroy our nation's most valuable institution—the family.

Chapter Five

The Specter of Sexual Abuse

There are few crimes more heinous than the rape of a child. To be falsely accused of such a crime comes close.

Shielded by immunity laws, people with an ax to grind may anonymously accuse any citizen of abuse, without fear of reprisal. Teachers, not trained as psychiatrists or physicians, are told that one out of every five children will be molested. Without sufficient expertise, they are encouraged to seek out these victims. Social workers, the majority of whom have never had a child of their own, are taught that all parents are potentially abusive, and to be suspicious of any display of affection between children and adults. In fact, the National Center for the Prevention of Child Abuse has called child abuse "'an American Tradition.'" Playing with children on the floor, bathing or showering with a child, cuddling, tickling, hugging, or even allowing a little girl to sit on her father's lap can be construed as sexual misconduct. A study conducted in Arizona revealed that facts used by CPS to substantiate abuse include such benign activities as

> accidental encounters of children with naked adults, bathing of four-year-old children by their parents, getting into bed with children (although nothing else is indicated), accusations by irate ex-landlords, ex-spouses, those who hate the family; skinny-dipping in the wilderness in front of less than two-year-old children. . . .

> In one case, the fact that the young, recently divorced mother slept in the same bed with her young son is used against her while the testimony

of the boy that nothing ever happened and that when he once got personal with his mother in bed she told him to, "Knock it off!" and sent him to another room, is buried and overlooked. Meanwhile, the State's efforts to achieve severance from her, over the boy's pleas and objections, continues. This is another of the penile plethysmography cases, justified by the CPS claim that the mother turned the boy into a future sex offender by being over-loving. [One of the Arizona cases where approximately one hundred boys per year, one-third of them between ten and twelve years old, were subjected to the horror of penile plethysmography—at the order of Child Protective Services (see chapter 6).][1]

There is something incredibly perverse about a system that believes that normal parental affection creates deviancy! It is perfectly natural for a young child, frightened by a nightmare, to crawl into bed with his parents. Only a filthy mind would believe that all such activities lead to sex. And, what parent has not forgotten to lock the bathroom door only to have a young child burst in with some exciting news? What kind of person believes that normal affection creates perverts, and pornography (used with the plethysmograph) creates normalcy? Yet, child abuse "experts" do not intervene with firms such as Farrall Instruments, who have children as young as five photographed naked, often in bondage or sexually explicit poses. After all, they claim, these pictures are sold for "therapeutic" purposes. But, what about the children who must pose for these? This is a blatant example of the double standard used by CPS.

Hugging too much or kissing a child on the lips during monthly visits were on Arizona's list of "categorically deviant behavior." Other events that were reported to the courts as noncooperative behavior by parents included showing emotion during visits, asking if the child is doing well while in state custody, or going to the press because the child is being molested in foster care. In one instance, a little girl asked, "Do you want me, Mommy?" The CPS worker reportedly refused to allow the mother to respond.[2] A Denver social worker confirmed that hostility or anger on the part of a parent over losing their child is considered a sign of guilt. If social workers had any knowledge of parent/child relationships, they would be more worried if a parent was not upset.

Falsely Accused

Every year, thousands of people are falsely charged with sexual abuse. No other crime carries such stigma. Even if they are acquitted, their lives are *never* the same. Anytime they are with a child, they are suspect. Survivors tell of being afraid to hug or hold children—even their own grandchildren. No one emerges unscarred. A large class action suit has been filed in Arizona against the state's Child Protective Services by families who have been torn apart by unjust, unproven charges. The following cases are just a small sampling of the problem.

Cindy and Michael Nemeth were concerned about the unruly behavior of their children, ages four and two. They turned for assistance to a La Frontera therapist. Since both parents worked, the therapist recommended a day care home, which would offer the children structure. A year later, the children began to act out sexually. The alarmed parents told the therapist, who assured them this was "normal" behavioral development. One day, their daughter recounted tales of satanic rituals, molestation, and physical abuse performed by a person wearing a wolf mask to the therapist. A short time later, the girl was abducted by CPS from the day care home, and the parents were blamed. This occurred in 1987.

Michael Nemeth was accused of urinating on his daughter and molesting her, although kidney failure and medications made it impossible for him to do either. However, this is another case, like the Wades', where CPS is determined to ignore the facts and nail the parent.

In 1990, the Nemeth's son told a different therapist that the abuse had been committed by the eighteen-year-

old son of the day care home operators. When that therapist contacted police with the information, they confirmed
that they already knew of such activities. In fact, CPS had
removed the granddaughter from the day care home after
she accused her grandfather of molesting her. Police investigation had also uncovered evidence of satanic wor-
ship in the home. The caregiver's husband was convicted
of child molestation and sent to prison in 1989, just three
years after the Nemeth's children had begun going to
that home.

Armed with this new evidence, the Nemeths approached CPS, only to be told that the facts were irrel-
evant to their case. Their daughter will only be returned
to them if Michael confesses that he raped his child. For
the last three years, Cindy has only been allowed to see
her daughter once a month, under CPS supervision.
Michael and the son have been allowed one supervised
visit per year, at Christmas.[3]

Danny and Dorthea Clevenger were concerned one
morning when their five-year-old had trouble urinating.
Thinking that she might have a bladder infection, they
took her to the hospital. To their horror, they learned
that the child had been raped and exposed to gonorrhea.

Angry, they confronted the young man in his twen-
ties who had baby-sat the girl the day before. When he
refused to answer their questions, they escorted him to
the police station. But, instead of receiving assistance, the
Clevenger's were rebuked for "kidnapping" the baby-sitter, and the man was allowed to leave without being
questioned. However, the police did call a CPS caseworker,
who immediately accused the father of perpetrating a
number of deviant acts upon his child.

Though David Clevenger tested negative for gonorrhea, CPS persisted in their claim that he was guilty.
Throughout the entire proceedings, CPS refused to question the baby-sitter or to ask that he be tested for the
disease. After a two-year battle, the couple lost all parental rights to their daughter. Eleven years later, they have
no idea where their child is or how she is faring.[4]

A six-year-old girl was abducted from her kindergarten class because an anonymous tipster saw the child rubbing herself between the legs. Once in custody, the child was subjected to a grueling, four-hour interrogation by two adults. As in most interrogations, the questions were leading and suggestive. When the little girl pleaded for them to stop and let her go home, the "professionals" tormented this child with comments such as these:

"You won't go home if he is gonna be there."

CHILD: "He's gonna pick me up."

"No he's not, no he's not."

CHILD: "He has to. He has to take me home."

"We're not gonna let you see him until we get all of this mess straightened out. Let me ask you this, is there anybody else there when these bad things happen to you?"

CHILD: (no reply)[5]

Up to this point, the child had repeatedly told her tormentors that her daddy had never done anything to hurt her, that he had never done any bad things. Throughout the entire ordeal they would lie about her previous responses to try to trick her into accusing her stepfather of molesting her. The child refused to fall into the trap. The examiners began to grill her in detail about various sexual acts he might have performed on her. The poor girl, who had no prior knowledge whatsoever about sex, stood firm in her denials. Finally, she described her father accidentally brushing against her one time when they had taken a shower. She made it very clear, however, that he was shampooing his hair at the time and did absolutely nothing sexual.

"Did you put soap on your body or did he?"

CHILD: "I did."

"Did he wash you at all?"

CHILD: "No."

"Did his part go inside your part at all?"

CHILD: "No."

"Was it rubbing up against you?"

CHILD: "No."

"No?"

CHILD: "But it touched me. When are you going to stop though?"

"Pretty soon, pretty soon. See, we have to know all the details so that we can make this stop, so that he doesn't touch anyone else, any other little girls. You wouldn't want him to touch another girl, would you?"

CHILD: (no reply)

Later:

"You said sometimes your mom touches your body parts when she washed you?"

CHILD: "Yeah, she does."

"Does your dad do that?"

CHILD: "No, just my mommy."

"Did you say earlier that he was rubbing against you?"

CHILD: "No."[6]

After enduring four hours of hostile questioning, the child still had not accused her stepfather. So, she was whisked off to the hospital where she was stripped by strangers, photographed, and subjected to a vaginal exam. The diagnosis: a yeast infection, something she had battled off and on all of her life. There was absolutely no evidence of molestation.

Nevertheless, the stepfather was arrested on a molestation charge. When he was released, it was on the condition that he move out of the home and have absolutely no contact with the girl. Charges have never been filed, yet three years later he is still living alone. He has been told that if he ever wants to go home, he'll have to "admit" molesting his stepdaughter.

The mother insists things will never be the same. "I've had to discuss sexual things with her that I never expected to have to talk about. Like in the interrogation they asked if he had put his penis in her mouth, so then she wanted to know why someone would do that."

"The damage they caused my daughter in a few hours has taken me years to remedy, and I'm not done yet."[7]

Children are repeatedly told by school officials that they have a right to control their own bodies—that no one has the right to violate their privacy. Just shout "No!" they're told. Yet, the child protective system, which promotes such programs, feels no qualms at all about kidnapping children, forcing them to be strip searched, examined and photographed nude by strangers without any loving adult support present, even when the children deny any abuse and beg to be left alone or to see a parent. All that is needed is an anonymous tip about "possible suspicion." Surely, this treatment is tantamount to system-imposed rape.

A Question of Custody

Molestation accusations have become so prolific in custody disputes that one attorney has referred to such charges as "the nuclear weapons of custody suits." State social workers in Washington credit the dramatic increase in abuse reports to an increasing trend among divorce attorneys to encourage abuse charges whenever custody or visitation disputes arise. This is what Ken believes has happened to him.

Ken thought he was in love. For five months, he and Sarah were constant companions. (Some names have been changed.) When Sarah discovered she was pregnant, she immediately withdrew from the relationship and let Ken know that she wanted him to have nothing to do with the child.

Fearing she would leave the state and he would never see the baby, Ken hired an attorney and launched a paternity suit before the baby was even born. He requested joint custody, asking that the child be allowed to live with the mother, but that he be given liberal visitation rights. He expressed a desire to be financially responsible for the baby and to be allowed to be a positive influence in its life. "You see all these kids in gangs," he said, "and most of them don't have a father. I didn't want that for my child."

Sarah's family, who had previously been very accepting of Ken, were put off by the suit. Worried that Ken might abduct the new granddaughter, the grandmother began to fight all visitation. Ken insisted that he would never take the child from its mother, yet the grandparents opposed the court-ordered visits.

Finally, Ken was granted three visits a week, and he thought the situation would stabilize as they all became used to the routine. However, one month later he came home from work to find a message from Social Services. He was being investigated for child neglect. Only at the hearing did he discover that the charge was molestation. It seems his daughter had developed another urinary tract infection. The examining doctor at Children's Hospital said the problem was caused by an underdeveloped valve between the kidney and bladder, a situation not particularly uncommon in little girls.

Still, the grandparents insisted Ken was to blame. From the very start the social worker assigned to investigate the case told Ken she thought he was guilty. His filing a paternity suit and seeking visitation was "highly suspicious," she contended, since the majority of single men never sought to take on such a responsibility. She canceled all unsupervised visits, and his three-year-old daughter was immediately assigned to a therapist.

The therapist engaged in "play-acting" sessions in which the little girl was encouraged to vilify her father. After ten months of "therapy," the girl supposedly accused her father of molestation. Whether or not this is true, Ken doesn't know. Though the therapist claims the incident was videotaped, neither he nor his attorney have been allowed to view the alleged accusation. Recently, all criminal charges were dropped.

The toll false accusations exact upon the children is immeasurable. In some areas, the proliferation of custody-related accusations has had a backlash effect. Judges who become disgusted with the use of such tactics begin to discount any divorce related claim. While this may help those falsely accused, it also forces children who are being molested to remain in a dangerous setting.

Another victim is the child who is unwittingly snared into making the accusation. A psychiatrist confided this story shared by a sixteen-year-old patient. When the girl was young, her parents had a bitter divorce. The child remained with her mother, but had been granted regular visitation with her father. One day her mother told her that her father was very ill, but that they would not let him into the hospital without the daughter's help. If the daughter would say that her Daddy did certain things, then he could get the help he needed. He would be so grateful, her mother assured her, that when he got out of the hospital, he would buy her a lot of presents, and they would have fun together again.

Sobbing, the teenager described to the psychiatrist how her mother had rehearsed the story with her. The girl was then taken to a doctor in another town where the family was not known, and she recited her speech. After that time, she did not see her father again. Years later, she discovered that her father was in prison, convicted of molesting her. From this time on, the relationship between daughter and mother went down hill. Later, during an argument with her mother, she learned of her father's suicide.

A short time later, the teenager came to the psychiatrist for help. She felt guilty and responsible for her father's death. Fearing for her well-being, he offered to arrange in-patient treatment for the hurting girl. She agreed, promising to call back the next day. But, it was too late. That night the distraught sixteen-year-old took her own life.

How many other children have been unwittingly snared into making false accusations? How many lives have been destroyed?

Fact or Fantasy?

When Phoenix Memorial Hospital came under fire for using penile plethysmography on boys as young as ten, the Sexuality and Addiction Program placed a two-page advertisement in the local paper to justify its actions. The ad began with a set of startling "statistics":

Fact: 1 in 4 females are sexually abused by age 18.

Fact: 1 in 6 males are sexually abused by age 18.

Fact: 1 in 5 children will be sexually abused by age 18.[8]

These same figures are used nationwide to encourage reporting and to campaign for even more money and power for CPS. The disturbing numbers came from a study by Diane Russell at Mills College in California. This study, however, was flawed in many ways. First, all of the subjects for Russell's study came from San Francisco, which does not give a demographically balanced sampling. Next, all of her statistics were derived from anonymous responses by adults to a questionnaire. There was no way to verify the data. But, the most blatant example of manipulation was her broad definition of abuse. "Russell defined sexual abuse as any touch that was viewed as unwanted or that could be construed as sexual in nature."[9] Included were unwelcome kisses from not-so-hot dates, being brushed against in line at school, or any accidental touch that might have been construed as sexual. Russell redefined these normal experiences as rape, and her shocking figures were born.

In 1990, Russell's conclusions were challenged in a study conducted by the U. S. Department of Health and Human Services. This study was based on nineteen American counties determined to be representative of the entire national population. Sexual abuse was defined from touching through clothing to penetration. These results were much different. They revealed that 1 out of 250 females (3.9 per 1000) suffered from some form of sexual abuse, with 1 out of 500 children, male and female combined (2.2 per 1000) were sexually abused.[10] In spite of the astounding disparity of these studies, Russell's study is popular in mental health and CPS circles.

Mental Health?

Therapy has become the pet cure-all of social service organizations. Often, guilty parties are allowed to retain their children as long as they will consent to "therapy." One man who admitted molesting his daughter regularly for several years never spent one day in jail. (The names of the individuals have been omitted to protect the identity of the victim.) Instead, he enrolled in CPS-ordered therapy. This man never showed any real remorse for his years of abuse, nor did he apologize to the child. He told his therapist that his only wrong doing was "perhaps a misuse of parental authority." The man described his actions as an "outgrowth of his love" and denied that he had harmed his child in any way. He claimed she had "wanted it" and had even been the instigator on many occasions, though she had only been eight-years-old when the abuse began. The daughter's version, however, revealed years of brutal beatings and rapes. Yet, the case was closed, and the child was ordered to remain at home with the abuser. After all, the insurance allotment for therapy had run out, so obviously the man was cured.

Some people choose therapy as a profession out of compassion; some are attracted to the power and money; and still others work in this area for their own perverse personal reasons. If a parent introduced an eight-year-old child to masturbation, they would be justly accused of sexual abuse. Yet, Kathleen Goodfriend, a family counselor, was allowed to force this information on Alicia Wade, to employ brainwashing techniques, to conceal evidence of the father's innocence, and to drive an innocent woman to attempting suicide—all in the name of mental health. These techniques are not unique to this case; rather, they are common complaints from survivors of such apparent malpractice. "Therapists" are the ones who are subjecting young children—many of whom had never been accused of a crime—to pornography, ammonia aversion therapy, and the sexual torture of penile plethysmography (see chapter 6).

Sex abuse counseling has become a billion dollar business. If an evaluation reveals that no abuse has occurred, the sessions—and money—end. However, therapists need only file a complaint form and a report to social services to tap into thousands of dollars from Victim Witness Funding. In California, this can run up to forty-six thousand dollars per client. In a separate program, there is designated funding available for attorneys who help file victim-witness claims, even if the claims are filed without the attorney's intervention, if the charge was acquitted, or was unfounded or dropped. In 1990, over $60 million was paid out in California alone.[11]

However, there are no funds set aside for victims of false accusations. There is nothing to reimburse them for the financial devastation, loss of reputation, loss of jobs, and sometimes even ruined marriages. Nor is there any way to compensate for the impact of forcible search and seizure, strip searching, intensive interrogation, and incarceration of the children who become victims of the state. When previously nonabused children are finally returned home, they often exhibit the symptoms of abuse. They may be fearful, withdrawn, stutter, develop tics, or exhibit violent behavior. Children exposed to explicit sexual information during the interrogation process may become eroticized.[12] Many have been abused in foster care.

The Herlachers are just one example among thousands. Their nine-year-old boy bruised his hip sliding into second base in Little League. Later that day, he received a spanking for not doing his chores. The next day, his bruised hip was sore, so the child asked to be excused from PE. He was sent to the school nurse to be examined. When she saw the bruise, she asked him if his parents ever spanked him, and he told her of the discipline the day before. The next day, he and his eighteen-month-old sister were removed by CPS from their home.

Paul and Sherri Herlacher were told that the children

had been removed because of the spanking. The Herlacher's explained that the hip bruise was not a result of the swat they had given their son but had occurred during a baseball game. To support their position, they even collected a letter from the coach confirming this fact. The CPS worker refused to look at it. They were told that Paul would have to move out if the children were to be returned. Frantic to get the kids, he complied. After two weeks, the children were returned to Sherri.

One month later, at a CPS office, Paul was accused of sexually molesting his little girl. It seems that the child had tested positive for chlamydia, a sexually transmitted disease, prior to leaving the foster home. The caseworker demanded that Paul and a family friend be tested for the disease. Both tests came back negative. The Herlachers then demanded that the foster parents be tested as well, since the child had been perfectly healthy before being snatched by CPS. Their requests were ignored. When the case reached the courts, CPS insisted that the test results were immaterial. The facts don't matter if they do not support the CPS position. Fortunately, the judge disagreed. The test results were considered proof of Paul's innocence.

Though no criminal charges had ever been filed against Paul, it took nine long, devastating months before the family was reunited. In the interim, Paul had been fired from his job because of the amount of time he spent going to court and CPS therapy appointments. (CPS is often criticized for being unwilling to accommodate work schedules.) His employer told him he could not return until his affairs with CPS were concluded.

Without a job, and with twelve thousand dollars in legal and counseling fees, the couple was financially devastated. Their savings ran out, their utilities were turned off, and they fell behind on their house payments. Their credit was completely destroyed.

Four years later, the family continues to suffer from the ordeal. "'The children still have not recovered,' said Sherri. 'They are still afraid that someone or something may come and separate us all again. Their fears have been very real to them.'" The question of how their daughter contracted chlamydia remains unresolved. "I have to live with the fear that she was being sexually assaulted while in CPS' custody, and I wasn't able to do anything about it. I have spent many a sleepless night over that issue."[13]

Building a Case for Abuse

Among the tools given to social workers to assist in ferreting out sexual abuse are Risk Factor Checklists which purportedly identify girls who are at greater risk for sexual victimization. David Finkelhor, described as an expert in this field, has included the following items as the strongest indicators of potential abuse:

Does the child have a stepfather?

Has the child ever lived apart from the mother?

Is the child not close to the mother?

Did the child's mother fail to finish high school?

Does the mother exhibit sexually punitive behavior?

Does the mother fail to give physical affection to the child?

Is the family income less than $10,000?

Does the child have two friends or less?[14]

While some of these factors may exist in abused children, there have been no control studies done to determine how frequently these same conditions affect children who are never molested. High school dropouts are not necessarily molesters, nor do they necessarily marry perverts. In fact, some self-confessed molesters are highly educated; nor does poverty necessarily affect morality. Why does shyness in a child indicate abuse? Unfortunately, some CPS caseworkers accept "risk factors" such as these to be sufficient proof for filing charges.

If a doctor announced that he had found a cure for

AIDS, yet his research had contained no control studies, he would be laughed out of his profession. Yet, such practices are common among sex abuse professionals. The incredible danger is that these theories are accepted as sufficient proof to destroy families and send people to prison. One such theory, called the Child Sexual Abuse Accommodation Syndrome, was introduced by Dr. Roland Summit. This theory proposes:

1. Children never lie about abuse.
2. An abused child will often deny abuse, therefore, denial is a sign of abuse.
3. To disclose abuse, a child must be surrounded by people who unequivocally believe the charges and who use supportive interrogation to keep the child's belief system intact.
4. All disclosures are to be believed as fact, no matter how bizarre or improbable the act.
5. All subsequent denials are part of the initial denial process.[15]

Summit further contends that if the alleged perpetrator denies the charge, then he or she is lying; she is in denial. While these may be symptoms of abuse, there is no accommodation in the theory for innocence. If a child alleges abuse, he is honest; if he denies it, he's a liar. No adult accused of abuse is ever considered innocent. Though Summit has since stated that his syndrome should not be used as proof for prosecution, that is exactly how it is being used.

A California psychiatrist, Dr. Summit worked primarily as a consultant with two agencies and appeared frequently in court as an expert witness. It is ridiculous to assume that his conclusions were not based upon his own theory. His Accommodation Syndrome has been widely accepted and is used as justification for suggestive, often hostile interrogation of supposed victims. Those who believe that no charge of sexual abuse is unfounded will go to great lengths to substantiate the claims. Suggestive questioning can be used for months or even years until the therapists get the results they are seeking. Many children, like Alicia Wade, are promised that they can only return if they will make an accusation.

Does child sexual abuse exist? Certainly. Should the victims receive competent help? Yes. But, there must be accountability in the process—something that does not exist now. Therapists should be supervised when dealing with children. One social worker, who has worked with many victims of molestation, also agrees that many charges are unfounded. According to her,

> the sex abuse cases are the hardest. Kids can be programmed into saying that they have been molested when they haven't. Therapists can suggest things, and the kids pick up on it. Then they make accusations that aren't true. Sex abuse cases are especially hard with teenagers, because teenagers can make up things. I know there are cases where someone else might have abused them and the kids are transferring it to the parents. And the kids may have made it up. So, it can be very hard to determine if abuse really occurred.

Good Touch, Bad Touch

For years, it was argued that children never lied about sex abuse because they were too unsophisticated to know anything about the subject, yet that is no longer the case. Prime-time television contains explicit sex scenes that just a few years ago would have been banned from most family theaters. A government-sponsored public service announcement on AIDS features an animated, cartoon-like condom package. Accompanied by action music, the condom leaps from a drawer, runs across the room, sneaks by a sleeping cat, and crawls under the covers where two people are obviously about to engage in intercourse. This commercial, also shown during prime time, is guaranteed to attract the attention of the very young and elicit any number of questions.

Schools have joined the media in its efforts to make even the youngest children sexually astute. Children enrolled in a preschool sponsored by Denver's public schools were offered AIDS education, subject to parental permission. Dr. Jocelyn Elders, Clinton's Surgeon General, believes that sex education should begin at the age of two. The most popular version of so-called sex abuse prevention programs has been based on the Good Touch, Bad Touch concept and often begin in kindergarten.

These programs utilize a "touch continuum," or a rating system for touching from *good* to *bad*. The assumption is that children would automatically sense the underlying purpose behind a touch. If it feels bad, it's abusive. If it feels good, then it's okay. But, this assumption is flawed. Children do not have the knowledge or sophistication to perceive sexual intent. Many pedophiles are adept at befriending kids, who in their innocence never suspect a thing until it's too late. Cordelia Anderson, who developed this concept, has changed her mind about the value of good/bad touch-based programs. She "now wishes she hadn't thought of it, since it oversimplifies the concept and makes it an easy answer to give kids; the majority of touch is, she now accepts, confusing."[16]

One of the immediate consequences of these programs is that children will often engage in play-acting situations after the classes. The curriculum also implies that children are in some measure responsible for their own safety. What about the child who has suffered abuse in the past? Is she to be made to believe that she could have prevented it by simply saying "no"? Other concerns expressed by parents are that the programs arouse a premature interest in sexuality. For many children, this is their first introduction to the subject of sex, yet it is presented as dangerous and frightening. This could have long-term negative effects, making it difficult for the children to develop normal sexual relationships later in life.

Perhaps the most harmful aspect of the program is that they teach children to be suspicious of normal parental affection—especially from their fathers. In a similar program held in an Adams County school in Colorado, the instructor told the girls that if their fathers kissed them on the lips or gave them a friendly pat on the rump, they were molesters. Many parents have complained that some children who have received this training begin to shun their parents, becoming fearful of normal parental affection.

The Family Welfare Research Group at the University of California at Berkely conducted a study of seven such programs for preschoolers. Their conclusions were that the children were too young, the programs worthless at preventing abuse, and that there were harmful side effects. "Before the programs were taught, all of the preschoolers reacted positively to descriptions of normal parent-child behavior such as tickling, bathing, and being tucked in at night. After the programs, between 10 and 20 percent showed signs of regarding the same activities negatively."[17] In an effort to protect our children, we are robbing them of their childhood. Young children have the right to trust their parents and feel secure in the safety of the family.

Ostensibly, these programs are subject to parental approval. Yet, literature that accompanies some of the programs warns teachers to be suspicious of any parent who objects, for that parent may very well be a molester. Because teachers are required to report any "suspicion" of abuse, some "parents who decline participation are suspected or even being reported and investigated for child abuse on the sole evidence of their refusal!"[18] There is no evidence that these programs have ever helped prevent abuse, yet they have been responsible for incredible damage to innocent families. This happened to a family in El Paso County, Colorado, after their ten-year-old daughter was shown a film on child sexual abuse at school. After the film was over, the children were asked if any of them had ever been touched in a private area by an adult. The young girl raised her hand and said her father had touched her on her bottom twice. As usual, the system acts first and asks questions later. Within twenty-four hours, she and two of her siblings were removed from the home.

Both the parents and the ten-year-old said that his "touching" had occurred on two occasions when the daughter had a rash and needed help applying the ointment. There was no evidence whatsoever of abuse. The younger children were quickly returned, but the older child was placed into foster care.

Although forbidden to call home, the child placed several frightened calls home to her parents. She told them the teenage sons of the foster parents were regularly forcing the older foster girls to have sex with them. Upset, the father called El Paso County Social Services, but they were unresponsive. "We take children out of homes so that they won't be molested; we don't put them into homes in order to be molested," they are reported as saying.

The parents finally regained custody of their daughter, but her childlike innocence had been shattered by the events she had witnessed while under the "protection" of the state. One month later, the foster home was closed when social service discovered that children indeed were being molested there.[19]

W. Allan Garneau, an educator for twenty-five years and an elementary school principal for twelve years, has watched the good/bad touch programs in action and believes that they should be eliminated. In his capacity as an educator, he has witnessed several tragic occurrences resulting from these programs, including the destruction of strong, innocent families.[20] One of the problems, he contends, is the emphasis placed on incest in most programs. The teacher's guild to the C.A.R.E. (Child Abuse Resource and Education) program actually states that incest is a very common form of abuse, yet research indicates otherwise. Most credible research indicates that one in one thousand children are victims of incest, and the majority of those cases involved someone other than the biological parent. Yet, the very same research indicates that thirty in one thousand children experience damaging reactions to the prevention programs![21]

Considering the antiparent bias of these programs, it

is only natural that they encourage children to seek help from teachers, police, and social workers, but not their parents. "Parents are rarely seen as useful allies in these programs, implying that parents are the majority abusers."[22] This emphasis has a very negative effect on family integrity.

Although these programs began with good intentions, Garneau concludes:

> To continue the proliferation of some of the programs we subject our children to is a betrayal. The loss of trust and closeness among a happy family cannot be justified on the basis that someone had good intentions.
>
> . . . In the meantime, the only reasonable step that school systems can undertake . . . is to place an immediate moratorium on all such programs.[23]

Physical Evidence

In many obvious cases of molestation the physical evidence is readily discernible. This may include torn vaginal or anal areas, presence of semen or even the presence of sexually transmitted disease. Some forms of sexual abuse do not involve penetration, or enough time may have passed for the child to heal. Dr. Woodland, a pediatrician, wrote an article about what doctors should look for in examinations for sexual abuse. Some of the items included were dilated vaginal openings, vaginal scars or adhesions, missing hymens, hymen thickened or thinned, and hymenal tags and scars. However, these indications were all based upon clinical work with abused children; no control study was performed to see if these features were present in nonabused children. In spite of this, his findings have been the basis of "expert" testimony in sex abuse cases.[24]

In a control study of girls who have never been sexually abused, J. McCann et al. found many of the same features that had been used to convict alleged molesters. The size of vaginal openings varied among individuals. In some cases, normal irregularities may be confused with hymenal scars. McCann also concluded that it was impossible to tell the difference between "normal asymmetry" of the hymen and a hymenal "tear." Dr. Lee Coleman, who reviewed hundreds of cases of alleged child sexual abuse, concurs with McCann's findings. He concludes that examiners, expecting to find molestation, may easily overinterpret data that is not scientifically verified. In the few cases in which second opinions were solicited, the conclusions often varied. Until more control studies are conducted, Dr. Coleman contends, it is a travesty of justice to use this evidence in court.[25]

Overinterpretation of results also applies to lab work. For example, common ailments can be misdiagnosed as gonorrhea of the throat. This actually happened to the family of a two-year-old boy of Arapahoe County, Colorado. The parents had taken the child in for a routine throat culture. When the test supposedly indicated gonorrhea of the throat, a social worker showed up at the home and snatched the toddler. The boy's father denied any wrongdoing and tested negative for gonorrhea, but Social Services refused to listen.

> The man wasn't allowed to see his son . . . and a social worker, who brought the boy home briefly to collect his Christmas presents, didn't even have a car equipped with the required carseat.

> Then social services came back after Christmas and said, "Sorry, we had the test redone, and the boy had the flu."[26]

If social workers were less inclined to believe that all parents were perverts, the test would have been redone immediately to confirm the results. Then, a family's life would not have been so irresponsibly interrupted.

The San Diego grand jury also concluded that molestation cases were difficult to assess, but that examiners were much too quick to assume abuse had occurred, in spite of any medical findings.

In many cases of sexual molestation, it is almost impossible to prove that it happened. Conversely, it is impossible to prove that it didn't happen. The way the current system operates, suspicion of molestation, what "might have been," is sufficient to sustain a true finding. The Jury has read numerous medical reports from the Center for Child Protection which invariably read, "no physical finding, but history consistent with molest." *The burden of proof, contrary to every other area of our judicial system, is on the alleged perpetrator to prove his innocence* [emphasis theirs].[27]

The Center for Child Protection (CCP), a private contractor service that performs medical exams in cases of alleged abuse in San Diego, was set up as a check and balance for the system. What it has become is a rubber stamp for CPS. CCP rarely rules out molestation because it "might" have happened. Under examination, the director even admitted that he was not "as good as some doctors at maintaining an objective outlook."[28] This lack of objectivity has "poisoned" the Child Dependency System in San Diego since CCP is also responsible for most of the training offered regarding sexual abuse. The grand jury contended that "in Alicia W., Esmerelda B., and other cases, patently erroneous testimony by members of the CCP medical staff played a significant and most disturbing role in the outcome."[29]

Abuse does happen, and the innocent victims deserve protection. But, the system designed to protect the innocent has become the greatest perpetrator.

Chapter Six

State- Sponsored Sexual Abuse

Most states mandate that sex offenders undergo evaluations to determine their sexual appetites and assess their risk to the public. However, many child protective agencies and juvenile courts have extended that requirement to anyone who is charged with any sexual misconduct against a child—even if there has been no adjudication of guilt. After all, any adult charged with abuse is automatically presumed guilty and must seek to prove his innocence. The results of these unproven, unscientific tests are then used as evidence against the person charged. However, if a person insists upon his constitutional rights and refuses to take the test, his refusal is seen as an admission of guilt. On this basis, he can be denied all access to his children. The current "assessment tool" of choice is a barbaric invention called the penile plethysmograph. This device, used on a daily basis in all fifty states, is an increasingly common means of assessing and treating adults and juveniles alike.

Penile Plethysmography

The penile plethysmograph utilizes a mercury-filled rubber ring connected to a computer which is used to check erectile arousal. An early version of this device was first used in 1908 to monitor drug reactions on dogs. Later, it was adapted for use by men who were battling impotence. Over the last twenty years, however, it has become widely used as an assessment tool for determining sexual deviancy, and in conjunction with other forms of therapy in treating sex offenders.

The bizarre test requires the "patient" to go into a booth, bare his genitals, and measure his penis. The subject then passes the measuring tape to a technician who selects the appropriate sized "strain gauge" (a mercury filled rubber ring) and attaches it to a computer monitor. The ring is passed back to the "patient" who must recline in a chair and put on the ring. (There is now a version available for women that consists of a phallus-shaped device which is inserted into the vagina.) Though no data exists to prove the accuracy of this meter, it supposedly monitors the level of sexual arousal that the person experiences during the so-called test. What follows next is the most perverted, debased, and exploitative display of pornography imaginable.

The most popular version incorporates slides of men, women, and children clothed, nude, and in various sexual poses. Kiddy porn is a major element, often showing nude children—as young as five—tied to beds, chairs, or other devices. Some show the children fondling each other; some picture children with adults; some have the children expressing fear; and others are described as playful.

Other therapists add a personal touch. After being accused of molestation in a domestic dispute, Chris Friend contacted a "counselor" to take the recommended sexual screening to prove his innocence and regain access to his children. After being strapped to this repulsive device, the counselor turned on a music soundtrack and began to narrate "a series of vignettes."

> One vignette dealt with a father performing oral sex on his daughter. In another, an adult male picks up several boys for sex. After every two or three molestation scenes, the counselor would throw in a vignette of normal sex. The counselor had told Friend to buzz him on the intercom after every story and tell him how he felt. But Friend, soon in tears, was unable to respond. The social worker, unmoved, warned him that if he didn't

give "the response we are looking for," sound effects would be added.[1]

The counselor who performed this atrocity, at a hefty fee of one thousand dollars per session, has contacted the navy requesting that he be hired to "treat" the Tailhook offenders.[2]

Other perversions utilize "homemade" pornography; videos of deviant acts including bondage, child molestation, homosexual and heterosexual episodes, and bestiality. Soundtracks may include screams and cries for help from women and children who are being raped or abused. Some evaluations include up to seven hundred true or false questions based upon an assumption of deviancy, such as:

> I get more excitement and thrill out of hurting a person than I do from the sex itself.
>
> I got the idea to rape while burglarizing apartments or houses.
>
> I have had sex with an animal.
>
> I have beaten a person during a sexual encounter.
>
> I have fantasized about killing someone during sex.[3]

Farrall Instruments

Until 1993, William Farrall was the first and only commercial manufacturer of the penile plethysmograph. When he opened his firm in Grand Island, Nebraska, in 1958, his primary business was the manufacture and sale of electronic metal detectors and diagnostic equipment to test cattle for brucellosis. But, times change, and when a therapist asked him to make a plethysmograph in the early 1970s, Farrall decided to diversify.[4] His firm is now the largest manufacturer of sexual "therapy" devices. The product line includes such bizarre items as "electric-shock devices, penis gauges, and pictures of nude little girls strapped to furniture-moving equipment."[5]

Questions regarding Farrall Instruments surfaced during investigations into a Phoenix Memorial Hospital sex abuse program that used Farrall materials in treating juveniles. Inquiries made to the FDA revealed that this product was not cleared by that department for marketing. "'Any medical device in this country has to be approved,'" stated Sharon Snider, a spokeswoman for the FDA in Washington.[6] Such approval requires two or three years of clinical studies demonstrating that the device is safe and effective, something that has never been done for the plethysmograph. However, there is a hitch. This law only applies to medical devices introduced to the market after 1975, and, if Farrall's claims are accurate, his instrument is exempt.

Science or Porn?

The material available through Farrall Instruments is by any definition pornographic in nature. One of their catalogs, obtained by federal investigators, advertises the following photographs (among others):

> "Misty & Pam—Misty is tied to furniture-moving cart. Perplexed and trying to get away. Pam is in garage with hands and feet tied. Also tied to a standing box spring mattress. Models are nude."

> Misty is described in the catalog as 5 years old; Pam is 12.

> "Barb—Model is tied on chair and on bed. Nude scenes. Some scenes show fright, others show playfulness."

> The catalog elsewhere describes Barb as 14.

> "Barb, Pam & Jeff—Clothed and seminude. Holding guns, chains and other weapons."

> Jeff, the catalog states elsewhere, is 8 years old. Other pictures . . . carry descriptions such as "poses

are very seductive and explicit," "child friendly and seductive," "close-up pictures of pubic areas."[7]

So, why isn't this trash banned? Sale and possession of child pornography is still illegal in America; yet, many therapists, hospitals, and social service agencies justify the use of these photos as therapeutic! Other items of interest are electric-shock implements used for behavior modification. "The Wireless Shocker" allows a therapist to torture his victim with eight hundred-volt shocks using a remote control and a device strapped around the patient's waist. A smaller version, the "Take-Me-Along-Personal-Shocker" is described as "ideal for carrying in the pocket or medical bag."[8]

However, Farrall Industries will not sell their items to just anyone. Only those willing to sign a form stating that they are therapists need apply. It seems no actual verification of the purchasers' credentials are required, however.

It is ironic that the same people who would intervene in a family because parents took pictures of a child playing in the bathtub would have no objection to nude pictures of children in bondage and sexually explicit poses used by therapists. While some counselors do express "qualms" about possible negative effects posing may have on the models, they still use the product.

Farrall claims that the child models (as young as five) are not harmed because the models used in his slides are nudists, and have a different perspective on nudity. In the case of minors, both the child and parent have consented, and the parent is supposedly present during the photo sessions. Whether or not this is true, no one seems to know, but therapists using the slides are quick to quote Farrall's twisted justification when questioned on the impropriety.

Even if this is the case, does it matter? What child is capable of making an informed decision about posing in such a manner? And, what kind of a perverted parent could allow such activities? Nebraska Assistant Attorney

General Herb Spears viewed one of the bondage photos and said, "I don't see how a child could consent to that or a parent could consent to that."[9] Yet, other law enforcement officials disagree. Richard I. Mesh, chief of the Maricopa County, Arizona, attorney's organized-crime and racketeering bureau is one of these. "'You have to look at the purpose,' he said, adding that the material is used as part of a recognized therapy. 'It's not being done *to* the child in a form of abuse,' Mesh said. 'The child is being asked to cooperate.'"[10] So what! Most child molesters could use the same defense!

Phoenix Memorial Hospital

The use of the penile plethysmograph came under great scrutiny in Arizona in 1992 when questions arose over a sex-abuse treatment program operated by Phoenix Memorial Hospital, which routinely used this device on young juveniles. The program had operated behind such an effective veil of "confidentiality" that few people actually knew it existed. But, a mother's desperate battle to rescue her eleven-year-old son from the house of horrors finally pierced the veil.

The child had been taken from his home at the age of six because of alleged "sexual inappropriateness" on the part of the mother. Though the mother was never formally charged with any wrongdoing and her therapist recommended that she retain custody of her son, the boy remained in foster care for five years. (Details of the mother's alleged actions are not disclosed; however, it is important to remember that CPS in Arizona has accused parents of sexual inappropriateness for bathing four-year-old children; allowing a child to crawl into bed with a parent, even if *nothing* remotely sexual happens; and accidental encounters of children with naked adults.[11] Obviously, CPS has different standards for parents than it has for those who operate within the child-abuse industry.)

Testimony in court revealed that the child had been

sexually molested in two of the foster homes, while under the "protection" of CPS. Finally, shortly before he was to be returned to his mother, a judge had him placed in the Sex Abuse Treatment Program at Memorial Hospital for a mental evaluation. The mother objected, but her concerns fell on deaf ears.[12]

Prior to his commitment, a Child Protective Services memorandum stated it was "collectively perceived by all parties that (the boy) is not currently seen as a serious danger to harm himself or others." The examination notes from Dr. James Campbell, the Phoenix program's medical director, concurred.[13] But, the treatment program quickly changed the child's behavior.

Though this child had *never* been charged with any sexual crimes, he was treated like a convicted rapist. He had never exhibited sexual deviancy; yet, he was forced to strip down, allow an attendant to connect the plethysmograph to his penis, and then view pictures of nude children in bondage poses. Traumatized by the event, the child refused to comply with any further "tests." For a week, he was also subjected to ammonia-aversion therapy, a program which required him to inhale ammonia three times a day.

The child began to fight back, his desperation revealed in a note he wrote crying, "I want out of PMH ples git me out. I want out [sic]."[14] The hospital responded by restraining the child, giving him forty-five milligrams of Ritalin daily and sedating him at night. The mother called the manufacturer of Ritalin, Ciba laboratories, and described the behavioral symptoms her son was exhibiting. The lab said the child should be taken off the medication immediately, but the hospital refused to comply.[15] The mother and her attorney appealed to Maricopa County Juvenile Court Judge James McDougall to stop the treatment. McDougall refused, but the appeals court ordered the testing to stop until a full hearing on the program could be held.

If anyone else had shown similar pornographic pictures to this child, they would have been charged with molestation. Yet, the state contended that the treatment was necessary because the child had been molested himself and had since molested another child. Yet, testimony in court indicated just the opposite. In a hearing before the commissioner who ordered the child transferred out of the program, testimony was given that "the boy was not diagnosed with any sexual-deviance disorders and had not been acting out sexual behaviors."[16]

Suddenly, Phoenix Memorial Hospital joined in the request that the boy be transferred somewhere else. The hospital told CPS that the child was violent and exhibited homicidal tendencies. Dr. Campbell, who just two months before had described the child as harmless, recommended that the boy be placed in a restrictive, in-patient hospital because "he continues to pose a significant risk to society."[17] One month after the child was rescued from this nightmare, he was finally returned to his mother. All reports indicate that his behavior has stabilized and that he is doing fine.

Damage Control

As soon as the transfer was made, Phoenix Memorial petitioned to have the hearing canceled as "moot." It was too late. By this time, the extensive press coverage had caught the attention of two state senators, Stan Furman and Matt Salmon. In an effort to save their lucrative program, the hospital hired a public relations representative and took out extensive ads in the local newspaper. In these ads, they used startling (and inflated) statistics to describe the horrors of juvenile sex abuse, explained penile plethysmography, and extolled the benefits of their programs. The hospital then went on to justify their use of child pornography with children.

> All of the models are members of a nudist colony. The unclothed juvenile models all had parental permission to have their pictures taken, and their parents were present when the slides were made.

Without these slides, it is extremely difficult, if not impossible, to measure the adolescents' attraction to potential victims of both sexes and several ages. Given the deviant sexual history of the patients, nothing in the slides is likely to impact their sexual development. They are already sexually developing in a deviant manner.[18]

But, this was not the case. The ad contained a number of other false assertions regarding the program. Testimony revealed that many of their victims had never committed any sexually deviant act. Several children, including the eleven-year-old child whose plight blew the lid off the program, were only in the program because they had been victims of rape. So, the hospital decided to "rape" them again with the plethysmograph. Eventually, the hospital admitted that it had treated children who had never been convicted of any sexual deviancy, but promised to change its operating directives.

Phoenix Memorial also contended that "in the past 5 years we have used the plethysmograph in some rare cases with juveniles under the age of 12. This has only been done when the offense involved penetration, coupled with either violence or coercion."[19] Once again, this was a lie. Testimony in the subsequent hearings revealed that one hundred juveniles had been treated there annually: *one-third* of them between the ages of ten and twelve. Once again, the hospital was forced to back down and admit that it had subjected *all* the boys who entered the program to the test.

The hospital also reiterated its policy of requiring the patient's consent and parental, guardian, or court authorization before administering the plethysmograph testing.[20] Parents and children, however, who had suffered at the hands of Phoenix Memorial shared stories of intense pressure, coercion, and blackmail. Though all agencies involved denied charges of coercion during the early investigation, Frank Sanders from the juvenile court finally admitted under questioning at the state congressional hearings that "some coercion" was used.[21]

Other Victims Speak Out

The hospital brought out a parade of past patients who praised the program. However, not everyone's experience was positive. One twelve-year-old girl was so traumatized that she attempted suicide. The girl was in CPS custody when she began to fondle her little sister. Her mother (now divorced) claimed that the girl had been repeatedly molested by her stepfather, and the touching which occurred between the sisters was "acting out" and a sign that the girl needed counseling to deal with her own rape.

Phoenix Memorial refused to treat the girl as a victim. They assigned her to group therapy where she was repeatedly told to identify herself as a rapist; that she could do nothing to change; and that she would rape again if given the chance. The therapists also required her to write and record a violent sexual fantasy that she was forced to listen to several times a day, each time inhaling ammonia to prevent sexual stimulation.

According to the mother, the child refused to identify herself as a pedophile.

> Therapists insisted that the girl was a rapist. The girl wouldn't admit that, but her therapists persisted until one day she tried to kill herself, the mother said.
>
> "They found her in the bathroom with a plastic bag over her head," she said.
>
> "At the beginning of the (group-therapy) meetings, they'd make her identify herself as a perpetrator. To this day, she's traumatized by it; she cries about it. They kept telling her she'd do it again and there was no way she could prevent it."[22]

Another couple voluntarily approached Phoenix Memorial when they caught their boys, ages eleven and thirteen, experimenting with oral sex. The boys had discovered some discarded pornographic magazines. After filling their minds with the images in these magazines, they had decided to experiment. The boys both insisted that the episode had involved mutual consent, but the hospital refused to believe it. Instead, they accused the older boy of forcing himself on the younger sibling and ordered plethysmograph tests. The older child was then exposed to more pornography as "therapy." This defies all logic.

The parents were naturally deeply disturbed by this approach and sought to move their son elsewhere. Then, the hospital, which brags that it only treats willing patients with their parents' consent, threatened to recommend that CPS take custody of the youngest son if they withdrew the older brother from therapy. The family, who had sought help voluntarily, now felt terrified and trapped.[23]

Other parents, fearing reprisals from CPS, asked to remain anonymous, but their stories revealed similar coercion and trauma. "'They did this to my son,' said one father. . . . 'He's still upset to this day over it. He has bad nightmares.'"[24]

> "I'm scared for my son," one woman said. "We gave consent (for the plethysmograph), but we also had no choice. They told us they'd send him to Adobe Mountain (juvenile institution) if we didn't."
>
> Adobe Mountain, a correctional facility run by the Arizona Department of Youth Treatment and Rehabilitation, houses about 340 boys whose crimes include assault, drug dealing and murder.[25]

In at least one other instance, a mother's outspoken complaints about the program were used against her as evidence that she was not cooperative and that her child should not be returned to her. When an agency has

possession of someone's child, they have the most powerful coercive weapon of all.

Conflict of Interest?

As criticism began to mount, Robert Emerick, director of Phoenix Memorial's Sexuality and Addiction program, began to draw fire. Prominent local child psychologists expressed outrage that Emerick, who has a master's
degree in education, was an uncertified lay therapist with
no formal training in psychology or the treatment of
sexual abuse and disorders. Furthermore, they claimed,
the hospital was using experimental methods never recommended for juveniles. Dr. John Woods, a psychiatrist and
medical director of the Pinal-Gila Behavioral Health Association, is a state-designated expert who was asked to
review the Phoenix Memorial program. Dr. Woods became so concerned over the program's treatment of children that he altered his association's referral practices.

> Basically, what you have is an extremely high-paid
> money-making operation that makes $30,000 per
> patient and every three months probably charges
> about $500 for a retest. And it's based on abso-
> lutely nothing. . . . We don't send kids there any-
> more, and we try to avoid having kids sent there.[26]

The program at Phoenix Memorial was indeed lucrative, though the hospital portrayed it differently. Most of
the children involved with the program were referred by
juvenile courts, Child Protective Services, Indian Health
Services, and tribal courts. Hospital sources admitted that
90 percent of the program's funding came from the government. With more than one hundred children a year
enrolled in the program, as well as doing assessments on
adults facing molestation charges, that's a lot of income.[27]
A three day in-patient assessment, which included polygraph and plethysmograph tests, cost fifteen hundred
dollars. In-patient treatment could run between four hundred dollars and six hundred dollars per day.[28] Many
patients were there for six to eight weeks.

"This is taxpayer-funded child abuse," Mary Chapman, the Arizona V.O.C.A.L. director charged. "I think they're a whole bunch of perverts over there."[29] Others agreed, including state senator Stan Furman. "At best, what is happening to these children is an unproven, offensive procedure. At worst, this is child abuse and torture under the guise of treatment."[30] Program director Robert Emerick responded in typical "child-saver" fashion, charging that the critics of the program were "co-conspirators" with rapists and child molesters.[31]

The charges were *valid*: Phoenix Memorial was being paid well to expose children to pornography. In 1991, CPS had placed ten children in the program—not all of them guilty of sexual abuse—for the modest cost of $192,000, and this only accounted for 10 percent of the juvenile patients for that year. The tab for the CPS referrals was mainly paid for with federal money—your tax dollars at work. The Arizona Supreme Court had paid out another $124,906 to the program for juvenile evaluation and treatment.[32]

Another lucrative source of referrals for the program was the Maricopa County attorney's office. It was this connection that resulted in accusations of "conflict of interest." Emerick is married to Maricopa County's chief sex-crimes prosecutor, Cindi Nannetti. Although Nannetti didn't personally make any referrals, her office does require plethysmograph testing as a condition of plea bargaining for adult child molestation defendants. And, Phoenix Memorial was the primary provider of the "service" in the area.[33]

Treatment vs. Torture

Experts were flown in by the hospital to describe the virtues of plethysmography. Dr. Gene Able, director of Behavior Medicine Institute of Atlanta, praised the device as "the cheapest, fastest way to break through the patient's denial." Farrall, the manufacturer, claims the instrument is the most accurate means of assessing the chances a person will reoffend. He pointed to its widespread acceptance among professionals for treatment of sexual deviancy. The plethysmograph is used in 168 juvenile sex offender programs and 227 adult sex offense programs nationwide. Additionally, private therapists in all fifty states and ten foreign countries utilize the instrument.[34]

Steven Jensen, director of a similar juvenile sex-abuse center in Oregon claimed that use of this pornographic treatment with children was acceptable because "it has been used on juveniles since 1979, and there has never been a documented case that has shown any harm at all."[35] Mr. Jensen had obviously not listened to the stories of the children traumatized by the Phoenix program. Even though pornography has been proven to be addictive, Farrall claims that there is absolutely no reason to think that a child would be damaged by viewing nude bondage scenes, even if that child hadn't been exposed to such behavior previously. "It's not a concern, because there have been no reported effects of anything negative. It's not going to give them ideas they're not going to get off TV."[36] Such rationale is unbelievable! Even television is not allowed to show "kiddy porn." If this were indeed the case, then why is it illegal for everyone except therapists to show such material to children? Perhaps these gentlemen should listen to Ted Bundy's final interview.

Not for Kids

Many therapists, however, expressed outrage that such experimental, unproven methods as the plethysmograph or ammonia-aversion therapy was being used on juveniles. Even practitioners who use such programs with adults said that they should never be used with prepubescent children. Toni Cavanaugh Johnson, a clinical psychologist who works with child sex offenders says use of the device with boys under fourteen is "unethical. We do not understand the physiological arousal . . . in prepubescent children. These kids get erections when they're scared, they get erections when they're angry."[37]

Still others denounced the use of the device altogether. According to Dr. Herschel Rosenzweig, a Tucson child psychiatrist, "There are a lot more appropriate, more reasonable and rational therapies. . . . We certainly don't want to further victimize a child who has already been victimized."[38]

Dr. Otto Bendheim, a Phoenix psychiatrist, testified, "I believe that penile plethysmography should never be used in children." Using this test and pornography on a child "will set in effect a chain of events which will destroy the child's confidence in adults and will damage his sexual orientation."[39] A Tucson psychologist, Dr. Seikin, even presented evidence from previous critiques of the program that using such photographs could cause a child to be sexually stimulated at a premature age and that using pictures of bondage and other illegal acts could even increase the risk that the child would develop deviant sexual behavior. He also noted that "there are case reports which have indicated that the stimulus materials used in aversion therapy have triggered instead of extinguished child molesting behavior."[40]

Phoenix Memorial Not Alone

The program at Phoenix Memorial shut down shortly before the hearings began, yet they are not alone in the use of controversial, unproven sexual "treatments" for children. In 1992, there were 755 juvenile sex-offender programs nationwide. Many of these programs are now treating children under the age of twelve. Most organizations use traditional group and individual therapy, but there is a trend among juvenile programs to move toward controversial, unproven methods. These methods include: (1) The administration of drugs such as Depo-Provera to inhibit deviant sexual drives. (2) Penile plethysmography, which is used in thirty-five states, in approximately 22 percent of the juvenile programs. (3) Aversion therapy, which involves the use of bad odors to condition patients against becoming sexually aroused to deviant material.

This therapy is used in forty-seven states and 26 percent of the programs. Many programs, such as Phoenix Memorial, use inhalants made from ammonia, a poison. Electric shocks are used on kids in eleven programs. (4) Masturbation therapies, which are among the widest used methods. These fall into two basic categories.

> Juveniles involved in masturbation-satiation therapy are instructed to masturbate repeatedly to climax while reciting a deviant sexual fantasy for an extended period of time. This is done in private, but the patient often must tape record the session and turn the tape into the therapist as proof that the therapy has been completed. The goal is to use repetition to bore the patient with the fantasy and extinguish deviant sexual desire.[41]

What is more likely to happen is that the person will become bored and will require even more violence in an effort to attain a level of excitement. These methods do not change the heart. Once again, Ted Bundy is a prime example of how this works. It is entirely possible that such programs will create large numbers of Bundys to prey on the public. The second form of masturbation therapy is not much better.

They call this help, and the taxpayers foot the bill.

> In masturbatory-orgasmic conditioning, or masturbatory training, a juvenile practices becoming aroused to an age-appropriate, consensual fantasy. The goal is to condition the patient to become aroused to appropriate fantasies. This method is used in 150 programs.[42]

These programs do not work, nor will they as long as they deny God's basic guidelines. "As a man thinketh in his heart, so is he," we are told in Proverbs 23:7. If therapists wish to stop juveniles from committing sexual crimes, then they need to help them redirect their thinking and stop filling their minds with trash.

Chapter Seven

The Foster Care Nightmare

Every day in America, an estimated 600,000 children are living away from their families, caught up in the morass of the social service system. These children are parceled out among foster homes, group homes, juvenile facilities, and mental wards. This amount has increased an alarming 63 percent over the last decade, and, if the rate of increase continues, there could soon be 750,000 children lost in the system.[1]

Of these, it is estimated 40 percent will never return home.[2] Over half of them will be away for one year or more, and the majority will have multiple placements—some, as many as fifteen temporary "homes."[3] Many kids will languish within the system until they reach eighteen, when they are turned out on the streets. They will be given a little cash, a bus ticket, and their personal belongings. Homeless, without personal ties or educational opportunities, their futures are in jeopardy. The system that is supposed to provide a better life for these children often does the opposite. Unable to form bonding relationships, many take to the streets. In Massachusetts, 60 percent of the state's criminals come from foster homes or state institutions. In California, that number is 69 percent.[4] Tragically, most of these kids do not need to be taken from their homes.

The rule of thumb for all CPS agencies is "to err on the side of the child." If there is any suspicion of abuse, social workers generally yank the child out of the home, often prior to any investigation. In this way, they claim, the child is at least protected. If the charges are unfounded, the kid can always go home, so no harm has been done. Hostility or anxiousness on the part of the

parent is considered a sign of guilt or psychiatric disorder. After all, the child is safe in the care of the state, so
what's the problem?

But, the children are *not* safe in foster care. In fact,
studies indicate that they are actually ten times more
likely to be abused in foster care than in their own homes,
something many CPS workers realize. The person who is
safer is the caseworker. If a child who is left at home is
injured or killed, then the caseworker may face disciplinary or possible civil repercussions. If a child is molested,
injured, or killed in foster care, the caseworker is free
from blame.

Another issue that CPS workers generally ignore is
that *every* child is traumatized by separation from his
parents, and such an action should *only* occur if a child
is in clear and evident danger. That guideline does appear in most CPS departmental regulations—a necessary
ingredient for receiving continued federal funding. A
commitment to "reasonable efforts" for family
reunification, as mandated by Public Law 96-272, also
receives lip-service. However, in actual practice, it is basically ignored.

Children need families. It is from family that a child
learns bonding, values, and a sense of self. The family was
the first institution created by God. Young children gain
a sense of safety from their perception that their parents
can protect them from all harm. When a child is abducted from his family needlessly, even for a short time,
his feeling of safety is shattered, and the consequences
can be far-reaching. According to Professor Ann Coyne
of the Department of Social Work at the University of
Nebraska in Omaha, "We have a tendency to want to
'save' children. We feel we're doing the child a favor [by
taking him away], though in fact we may be disrupting his
development enough that it can affect his ability to learn."[5]

Bonding is a necessary ingredient in cognitive, emotional, and behavioral development. Ripping a child from
his family can cause serious side effects. Studies show that
breaking family bonds in children ages six to eight can

cause short-term memory loss and may affect their ability to read. Professor Coyne believes that many of the children in foster care labeled "learning-disabled" actually became disabled due to the separation and lack of bonding.[6] Emotional development is hindered when children lack a sense of history. Loss of parents can cause incredible grieving that results in negative and even violent behavior. Children who bounce from placement to placement can experience rapid mood swings from anger to depression. Every time the child is moved, grieving starts again, and the child withdraws and becomes even more detached. One ten-year-old boy who had been placed numerous times said "I wanted to die, because if you die, you don't have to start all over again."[7]

There is a public misconception that placement only happens in cases that involve serious allegations and then only after careful investigation and review, but nothing could be further from the truth. Placement depends strictly upon the whim of the individual caseworker in the field. In many cases, children are placed into state care simply because an anonymous tip came in on Friday afternoon, and the caseworker assigned wanted to get home for the weekend. If a child is young, he is yanked out of the home faster. Even though younger children are more traumatized by being forcibly removed from their families, they are seen as more vulnerable to abuse. Unfortunately, they are also more vulnerable to abuse in foster care. Judges who rule on such placements spend an average of three to eight minutes per case on the first hearing, hardly time to hear arguments or even examine the appropriateness of the placement. Essentially, this is just a rubber stamp process.

A San Diego grand jury confirmed that once the decision for placement has been made, the investigation is conducted "with a bias toward finding facts to support detention or removal and reports only that information which justifies detention."[8] Retaining possession of a child only requires a "preponderance of evidence," not "beyond a reasonable doubt." "As a practical matter, evidence contrary to DSS' (social service) position is either excluded or ignored. DSS may weave its case with hearsay evidence and the speculation of 'so-called' experts. More than 98 percent of all petitions [in San Diego] are granted."[9] The grand jury denounced the DSS claim that this percentage was based upon their expertise in only filing necessary petitions. One witness stated that investigating caseworkers "don't know the difference between opinion and evidence."[10] Concurring with this opinion, the jury wrote: "Child Protection Services cannot distinguish real abuse from fabrication, abuse from neglect, and neglect from poverty or cultural differences."[11]

In many cases, therapists and social workers have actually lied in court to support their case, yet no disciplinary action was taken by the department. Others have blatantly disobeyed court orders that did not agree with their personal agendas, and no action was taken. Therapists are handpicked by caseworkers from a list approved by the department. As long as they agree with the social worker, their testimony is heard. If they disagree, their recommendations may never even be included in reports to the court. Some therapists express concern that failure to follow the department line on evaluations could result in their being removed from the list.[12]

Foster Parents

Being a foster parent can be a difficult commitment, and there are some very loving foster families. Children placed in these homes may have suffered from abuse or neglect and might have behavior problems as a result. All of the children are lonely. Many have been shuttled from home to home for so long that they have stopped bonding with any adults. This has been compounded by the practice of removing children from a placement simply because they have grown close to the family. Older children may have been placed in the system because of delinquency or because they have inflicted abuse on another child. Families with children may be placing their own kids at risk. Foster parents also find themselves susceptible to false accusations.

These concerns, as well as frustrations over dealing with CPS, tend to drive good foster parents away. During its investigation of the San Diego Department of Social Services, the grand jury found "evidence of foster care licenses being threatened and children being removed from foster parents who took a position in opposition to the department. The department bemoans the lack of good foster parents and yet loses them on a regular basis because of the way in which social workers treat them."[13]

Double Standard

The majority of foster homes, however, are terribly inadequate. A survey conducted by the National Foster Care Education Project in 1986 found that foster children were ten times more likely to be abused than children in the general public.[14] A 1990 study confirmed that the situation has not changed. Children have been beaten, starved, neglected, raped, and killed in foster care, yet nothing changes. CPS continues to ask for more money and more power to cure all the inadequacies. Time has revealed that throwing money at a problem does not make it go away. According to Susan Carter, executive director of the National Association of Foster Care Reviewers, "The foster care system is morally and politically bankrupt."[15]

Conditions that are grounds for removing a child from his biological home are often overlooked in foster settings. Foster parents receive more than twice the funds per child than a family receives on AFDC. When a home is overcrowded or messy, if the utilities are shut off, or if a family lacks "adequate" food, clothing, and shelter (whatever that may mean), the child is generally yanked out of the home and placed into state care. If complaints are lodged that a foster home is lacking in beds, food, utilities, or other necessities, CPS asks the public to be tolerant and decries the pitiful amount of money given to reimburse foster parents.

CPS is required to investigate all hotline calls. On the basis of an anonymous tip, they demand entrance into homes, abduct children from schools, and reek havoc in families' lives. Complaints about abuse in foster homes are also supposed to be reviewed, but, once again, the individual prejudices of the caseworker come into play. There is a natural preference for the foster parents over the natural parents, and, if a complaint about abuse or neglect comes from the natural parent, it is often disregarded. Because of the lack of placement facilities, behaviors that would not be tolerated in a natural home are sometimes overlooked. Also, to add insult to injury, CPS sends the bill for foster care to the parents—even when the child was taken without justification.

Information regarding the system's failures also comes from people working within CPS. In 1988, social workers from Oregon went public with some of their complaints as well. "It is ironic that some children are in equal or more serious jeopardy after they become wards of the state," the Cumberland County Caseworker Committee wrote. At that time, 150 children who were officially in state custody were actually living on the streets, in abusive situations, or in institutions. The examples they listed include:

> an eleven-year-old girl who was living on the streets;
> a thirteen-year-old boy who had been moved over twenty times in foster care and was now living with an older man, and possibly engaged in prostitution;
> a sixteen-year-old boy who had completed a jail sentence but was required to remain there for lack of a better place;
> a pregnant, sexually-abused seventeen-year-old who was living with an abusive male prostitute.[16]

The Money Motive

Child-savers inevitably claim that people do not go into foster care for the money, yet that is precisely the reason many inferior homes are in the system. Reimbursement varies from state to state, but, on the average, foster parents receive close to $300 per month, tax-free, for each child. Many homes have several children, which can bring in a sizable income. The San Diego grand jury reported: "For many of these foster parents this is a livelihood, and foster parenting has become another part of the child abuse industry. Foster care was referred to by one witness as the 'largest cottage industry in America today.'"[17]

Denver Attorney Larry Pozner, who represents families and foster children, encountered one foster home that had taken in so many children that two of the older kids were required to sleep outside in tents.[18] Other children report sleeping on mattresses in hallways and attics. Ostensibly, the money received is to reimburse the family for the cost of the child's care, yet that money is not always spent appropriately. Some children have been returned home with lice, sick, in worn-out clothing, and underfed.

A fifteen-year-old girl was placed into a foster home with nine other residents after she received a bruise on her arm in an argument with her mother. This foster home was receiving almost three thousand dollars a month for the care of these kids, yet the girl recalls, "We were allowed one three-minute shower every other day and three sheets of toilet paper whenever we had to go to the bathroom."[19] A grandmother tells of buying new school clothes for her granddaughters who were in foster care. When the girls were transferred to the next home, they were still wearing worn-out clothing that was a size too small. The foster mother had sent the new outfits to her nieces. Reports from the second foster home also indicated that the girls had been beaten with a belt in the first home, but this information was not passed on to the parent until much later, after the girls were returned.

Foster Parents vs. Natural Parents

There is a natural antagonism that often exists between foster parents and natural parents. Foster parents may view the natural family as inferior. Persuaded by caseworkers that the family is to blame for the placement, they are often asked to act as detectives, seeking evidence to corroborate the CPS charges. Many people become foster parents as a step toward adoption. In California, these are called fost-adopt homes. While there is nothing wrong with foster parents adopting children, it may create a conflict of interest if a child is placed in such a home before parental rights have been relinquished or severed. This was part of the problem in the Wade case. The first foster parent reported Alicia's testimony, which exonerated the girl's father. The caseworker responded by quickly moving the girl into a fost-adopt home that was interested in adopting her. In such a situation, it is only to be expected that the would-be adoptive parents would be less than cooperative regarding family reunification.

Alienating the Family

Caseworkers and foster parents may further alienate the family by discouraging visits. Placements may be so far from home that it makes visits almost impossible for parents who must depend upon public transportation, especially if two or more siblings are taken and are placed in different facilities. Some foster homes use visits as a reward or punishment to manipulate the behavior of the child; caseworkers may do the same to force the parents to conform to a treatment plan. One caseworker explained:

> If a child goes to visit their parents, and they are really upset afterwards, then the social service workers insist that the visits be cut off. Now tell me that makes sense! And the workers who feel this way the most are the ones who don't have children of their own. They say,

> "Now, Timmy came away from the visit screaming and crying." Well, wouldn't you? But this is seen as negative. His mother is really upsetting him, so visits should be terminated. But logic should tell you that you are separating a mother and her child, and if they are attached at all, this is a natural result of the separation.

Federal law requires that "reasonable efforts" be made

to preserve families in order to continue receiving funds, but this is rarely enforced. Caseworkers are required to submit reunification plans, yet these are often designed for failure. Termination of rights is often the goal from the start. During the San Diego investigation, "judges and referees were observed, seemingly without thought, ordering parents into programs which require more than 40 hours per week."[20] Many of these parents depend on public transportation, which may not accommodate all of the required appearances. Also, parents cannot complete the plans if they are trying to work. Yet, failure to comply with any element of the plan can be sufficient to terminate all parental rights. Testimony given by attorneys, therapists and social workers confirmed that "some of these plans are intentionally made impossible, particularly when infants or toddlers are involved."[21]

One mother, caught up in this cycle, shared her testimony. She was indigent and dependent upon city transportation, yet her children had been placed in four different sections of the county. Her reunification plan called for her to visit each child once a week, attend parenting classes, attend Alcoholics Anonymous daily, and go to both individual and group therapy. Her children had been removed for neglect, but while she was running the ropes laid out by CPS to restore her family, they were being brutalized by the state-chosen foster parents. Two of her children were sexually abused and one was physically abused. She told the jury, "They took my beautiful children and returned broken dolls."[22]

Abused by the System

Tales of abuse and molestation in foster care are common. Complaints were filed against a group home in Arizona that refused to feed the kids properly. Children were given one slice of toast for breakfast and chastised for asking for second helpings. One eleven-year-old boy placed there lost four pounds in just two weeks. Threats of jail and various punishments and withholding food were used as disciplinary measures.[23] Babies have been

returned with diaper rash so bad that they were in danger
of scarring. A Denver caseworker said,

> Except for the very worst cases, I try to keep the
> children home because our resources are so inad-
> equate. I had a case where the two younger kids
> were in a foster home and they were tied to a bed
> and abused. Another child was placed in 5 homes
> and abused in 4. We finally sent him home be-
> cause we were messing up worse than his family
> had.

Foster children seem especially susceptible to sexual
abuse. Child molesters gravitate to positions of authority
over children, and a foster parent has a great deal of
power over lonely and frightened wards. If evidence of
abuse appears, they can always blame it on the parent.
With the obvious bias against parents, they may be readily
believed. Additionally, it is easier to threaten a child into
silence if he knows a person has the power to prevent
him from ever seeing his family again.

County agencies are constantly concerned about publicity and liability and may quietly close homes that should
be prosecuted criminally. There are foster parents who
get closed down in one county for suspicion of sexual
abuse, and they simply move and set up business in another county. This has happened recently in a western
state. A foster home was shut down for allegations of
sexual abuse. When they applied in another county, the
placement agency called the previous county and asked,
"What is this man like?" The county official responded,
"We closed him down as a foster home," but would not
disclose why. So, the placement agency picked him up.
The man is now facing charges of molesting several children in the second county. Something is wrong with a
system that is more interested in protecting its image
than in protecting the children.

In Arizona, CPS is being sued for taking two sisters,
ages seven and eight, from their natural parents and placing them in a crowded foster home where they were
molested by the foster parents' seventeen-year-old son.[24]

In another state, a child was assaulted in foster care. Though the state was informed of the event, nothing was done. Four months later, the foster father sexually abused the child.[25]

A sixteen-year-old boy was assigned to a home with a single, homosexual foster father. The terrified boy told his caseworker that the foster parent walked around the house nude, asking the teenager to hug and kiss him. Upon investigation, the social worker discovered that there had been reports of sexual inappropriateness in this foster home for sixteen years, but nothing had been done. Anyone who opposed this person as a foster parent was called "homophobic." The department was not willing to let the caseworker make a change in placement. Next, the caseworker attempted logic, a tactic often lost on CPS agencies. "How can we allow this man to have teenage boys when he is attracted to males?" the worker asked. "Would we place teenage girls with a single, heterosexual male foster parent?"

After a while, the foster parent began complaining to the caseworker that the teenage boy was not giving him enough hugs and exhibiting enough affection. This was so unnatural. Teenage boys don't hug their own fathers that often, so why would a stranger expect that kind of treatment? Desperate, the caseworker finally turned it into a liability issue, asking the CPS supervisor, "What if a parent finds out a bit of this information and goes to the press?" At last, the home was shut down, but the closure is being appealed by the foster parent. No heterosexual foster parent would have survived sixteen years of accusations without any investigation. Yet, as the frustrated caseworker concluded, "The department is more worried about his rights than they are the kid."

As the system becomes more crowded, the rate of abuse in foster care continues to rise. When several lawsuits were filed in Illinois over mistreatment of foster children, the state argued that after removing the children from their own families where abuse was suspected, the Department of Children and Family Services has no

legal responsibility whatsoever for their mental well being. In addition, they only accepted responsibility for the
physical welfare of children placed in state institutions.
Those placed in foster care or private facilities were put
there at their own peril.[26] This is incredible! If state child
protection agencies will not accept responsibility for the
children it arbitrarily seizes, then it should be stripped of
all authority in family intervention. Until the child abuse
industry accepts responsibility for its actions—something
it is always demanding that parents do—then children will
continue to be abused.

A comprehensive study of foster-care abuse in Balti-
more helped reveal the extent of the problem. Based on
a study of social services' own records of 149 cases, forty-
two of the children, 28 percent, had been abused in foster care. Some of the incidents uncovered by the reviewers included:

> A foster parent who repeatedly hit a child with her
> fists, and left a child who could not control his
> bladder in his urine-stained clothes, even sending
> him to school that way. Less than a year later, a
> second child with the same problem was placed in
> this same home.

> A home in which "street-smart teenagers" were
> placed with foster parents aged sixty-seven and
> seventy-four. While the parents were asleep, one
> of the teenagers sexually abused younger children.

> A home in which the foster mother fondled the
> foster children and the foster father had oral and
> anal sex with them. At least one child remained in
> the home for four months after abuse of other
> children was discovered.

> A home in which the foster father severely beat a
> child with a belt and an extension cord. The child
> was not removed until two months after the abuse
> was discovered.[27]

Family Preservation

More money will not solve the foster care woes, nor

will it bring the child abuse industry into conformity with
the law. Public Law 96-272, the Adoption Assistance and
Child Welfare Act passed in 1980, was an attempt to stop
the flood of unnecessary out-of-home placements and to
preserve families. It intended to reverse the funding incentive for foster care by requiring that "reasonable efforts" be made to keep the family together. The act speci-
fied that removal of children should only occur when it
is absolutely necessary. If removal was necessary, the child
should be kept near home and visitation encouraged in
the "least restrictive" setting. Plans were to be laid out for
family reunification, with specific treatment and actions
lined out for the parties involved. Reviews should take
place at least every six months to make certain the family
is reunited as quickly as possible. Within eighteen months
of the removal of a child, there is to be a hearing to
decide permanent placement.

However, these requirements have been blatantly cir-
cumvented. Though leaders within CPS decry a lack of
funds, that is not the problem. The underlying reason
behind this failure is the philosophy of the child protection system. To preserve the family, you must believe in
it. CPS does not. These agencies are zealous in their war
against parental authority, preferring to reserve total power
over our next generation for themselves. All parents are
flawed, they claim. Abuse occurs in every home. Family
preservation is costly, philosophically flawed and will not
work. But, these arguments have been proven false. Family preservation is a cost effective, highly successful alter-
native.

A Family-Based Philosophy

Family preservation represents a radical departure
for popular child-saver mentality. This method views the
family as an indispensable entity, assumes that most parents truly love their children, and that a child is better off
in his own home whenever possible. These programs do
not advocate leaving children in dangerous situations;
rather, they attempt to modify conditions in the home so
that it will be at least as safe as removal.

To accomplish this, family preservation services are four-to-six week, in-home programs of intensive counseling and other services with families that are in imminent danger of having their children removed. Therapists, who are on call twenty-four hours a day, work with no more than two families at a time. At the beginning of the intervention, the therapist and family meet in the home to discuss the problems that have led to the crisis. Rather than dictating a treatment plan, like traditional caseworkers do, the therapist assists the family in setting its own goals. Therapists do not attempt to make the family into perfect models, nor do they try to solve all the problems. Instead, they attempt to give the family skills to solve their own problems and meet their own needs.

In families where there is a substance abuse problem, they confront the addicted member or members, help them enroll in treatment programs, and even attend meetings with the person to make certain that the program fits the person enrolled, making him as comfortable as possible. If the problems in the home are poverty issues, they assist the family with cleaning, getting help for utility bills, and job placement skills. Parent-child relationships, goal-setting, chore charts, and problem resolution skills can be taught much more effectively when the family is on its own turf.

Unlike most CPS workers, preservation therapists do not automatically assume guilt. Instead, they treat the family with respect and try to see what can be accomplished rather than placing blame for what might have happened. Most sociology classes teach that people are programmed by their environment from early childhood and simply cannot change. It's this philosophy that is embraced by traditional child-savers. That is one of the reasons that they are eager to assume guilt, to make impossible reunification plans, and to push for severing parental rights, especially if the child is young. They feel superior to the families they work with and feel no qualms about dictating changes to others that reflect their own personal prejudices.

Family preservation workers reject this unfounded and ridiculous assumption. They do not believe that a home must be "perfect" in order for children to thrive. They feel love is more important than an immaculate home and strict schedule. They believe that everyone is capable of change, and they attempt to help the family accomplish its own goals, rather than to dictate goals to them.

These radical differences in philosophy are undoubtedly why Child Protection Services and foster care are such dismal failures and family preservation programs are so successful and cost effective. One year after receiving preservation services, 80 percent of the families are still together. Based on surveys of all families served nationwide, the median cost of family preservation is $4,500 per family, while the median cost of foster care is $17,500 per child.[28] Costs of placing children in institutional settings can run up as high as $100,000 per year.

A Brief History

The first family preservation service, Homebuilders, was started in 1974 by two child psychologists, Jill Kinney and David Haapala. They decided to try working in a home before children were removed, a novel approach which is now being duplicated in thirty states. Michigan has the largest statewide network of family preservation services in the country, called Families First. This initiative began in 1988, and in the first four years five thousand families, including twelve thousand children, were served. Follow-up studies have consistently shown that 80 percent of the families have remained together. In the first three years of the program, the rate of increase of foster care slowed, but by the fourth year, foster care placements actually declined. Michigan is attempting to use Families First as a means of converting its child welfare system from a child-rescue system to a family-focused system. Because of the incredible cost difference, Families First has already had a positive budgetary impact.

Resistance to Change

In spite of its obvious superiority to the bankrupt foster care system, family preservation has received a great deal of resistance. Many social workers resist referring clients to family-oriented care because they do not value the family. Foster care and abuse counseling have become billion dollar industries—family preservation threatens this. But, the ultimate opposition comes because this program is not compatible with the agenda being pushed by most child protection experts: making all children wards of the state.

Chapter Eight

Tampered Witness

Cases of abuse quite often hinge on the testimony of very young children. For centuries, a child's credibility has been considered highly suspect. Several people lost their lives in Salem because of the bizarre accusations brought by young girls, many of whom recanted their testimony years later. From that time until the 1980s, small children were seldom allowed to serve as witnesses.

This reluctance naturally created a problem when the victim of the crime was young. For example, in cases of molestation, there are seldom eyewitnesses. In an effort to crack down on abuse, this attitude has been reversed, and an increasing number of preschoolers are testifying in court, on cases ranging from abuse to murder. To make the experience less intimidating, courts have waived many rules regarding testimony, allowing videotaped interviews—without any cross examination—and even hearsay testimony. Prosecutors are allowed to coach the young witnesses by asking leading questions. In many cases, children are banned from courtrooms, and therapists or social workers are allowed to offer uncorroborated testimony on their behalf, something that would *never* be allowed in any other arena. In essence, the accused is stripped of his constitutional right to due process. "Believe the children," we are told; but how believable is the testimony after it has been tainted by coercive, misleading, and often brutal inquisition from crusaders who believe that every anonymous tip deserves a guilty verdict?

Can Children Be Misled?

Numerous studies have been conducted since 1900, testing the suggestibility of children and their reliability as witnesses. Early tests indicated that children who were allowed to freely recall events were the most accurate, but, when leading questions were used, the answers were often inaccurate. And, once an erroneous response had been made, the children would often incorporate that response into their memories.[1] A German psychologist, O. Lipmann, observed that when children are questioned by adults who have authority over them, they are highly likely to tailor their answers to the perceived expectations of the questioner. The continual repetition of the same questions also puts undue pressure on children. If they are asked the same yes/no questions repeatedly, they get the impression that they must have given the wrong answer, and they will adjust their response accordingly.

Because of the increasing use of minor witnesses, it is important to determine how easily they may be misled and what methods of questioning are most likely to get accurate results. The current philosophy among child-savers and therapists involves "supportive questioning." In practice, this means coaching a child, sometimes for months, until the therapists gets the desired results, then quickly videotaping the testimony. Techniques used include blackmail (you won't ever go home unless you say your daddy did this to you), intimidation, threats, rewards, name calling, promises (you will get to go home; you will feel so much better; we will leave you alone when you tell us what we want to know), brainwashing techniques (having the foster parents tell the child her father is a rapist every night when she goes to bed), leading questions, lying about the child's previous answers, and convincing a child that all of his or her friends have made the accusations, so they may as well agree. These methods violate every rule of evidence, and, if used on adults, who are actually more likely to withstand this intense pressure, they would be thrown out. Yet, this is documented, standard fare for interrogating young children.

Stephen J. Ceci et al. conducted a series of tests on the suggestibility of children. For one month, a character named Sam Stone was described to a group of three- to six-year-old children as a clumsy person who always broke things that did not belong to him. After this period of indoctrination, a person claiming to be Sam Stone actually visited the nursery school where he spent two minutes with the children during a storytelling session. While he was there, he did not behave clumsily or break anything.

The following day, the class was shown a ripped book and soiled teddy bear. While no one actually accused Sam, "25 percent said that *perhaps* he had done it." For the next ten weeks the children were interviewed for two minutes each, once a week. During this time, they were asked two leading questions such as "'I wonder whether Sam Stone was wearing long pants or short pants when he ripped the book?' or 'I wonder if Sam Stone got the teddy bear dirty on purpose or by accident?'"[2] At the end of the ten week period, a different interviewer came to the class and asked the children to describe what had happened the day Sam Stone had visited. The results were impressive.

> Seventy-two percent of the 3- and 4-year-olds said Sam Stone had ruined at least one of the items in question (book or bear). When they were explicitly asked,

> Forty-five percent of the 3- and 4-year-olds replied that they actually had seen him do these things, as opposed to merely being told he did. These false accounts often were embellished with perceptual details. (Sam Stone took a paint brush and painted melted chocolate on the teddy bear; Sam took the book into the bathroom and soaked it in warm water until it fell apart) or emotional details (Sam was acting very silly when he spilled coffee on the bear; Sam was mad and ripped the book with his hands).[3]

Older children and control groups who did not receive information about Sam prior to his visit had fewer inaccurate answers, yet several still made false claims. Other tests were conducted, using varying degrees of misleading questions, as well as tests which involved sexually suggestive actions such as being kissed while taking their bath. These also revealed that very few examiners were capable of asking neutral questions, even when instructed not to lead the witnesses. And, those examiners who were given erroneous information about the stated event were even more prone to question children in such a way as to get the responses they desired. The tests confirmed that children want to "get the right answer," and are easily intimidated into changing their responses to please the examiner.

Clark-Steward, Thompson, and Lepore conducted a study of five- and six-year-olds during which a man posing as a janitor entered the classrooms and either cleaned the toys, including a doll, or played roughly with the doll. "Chester," the janitor, would talk with the children, and his conversation confirmed what he was doing with the doll. When the children were questioned later by a neutral investigator, their answers were consistent with what they had actually seen happen. But, when the first interviewer asked questions which contradicted what actually happened,

> 75% of the children's remarks were consistent with the examiners' script, and 90% answered the interpretive questions in agreement with the interviewer, as opposed to what actually happened. When questioned by parents immediately following the interview and one week later, children's answers reflected the interviewers' interpretation of the events. When the second interviewer contradicted the first interviewer, the majority of children fit their stories to the suggestions of the second interviewer. Moreover, children's subsequent reports to their parents reflected a mixture of both interviewers' interpretations.[4]

Other studies were conducted to see if young children were capable of lying. Ceci commented "that children are found to lie at times ought not surprise anyone, save the rather extreme advocates who have made such baseless claims." But, these "extreme advocates" are the ones who are in control of CPS, and courts want empirical data, not experience. Once again, the tests proved the obvious. Children will lie if they are afraid of disapproval, wish to escape punishment, are promised rewards, or for a variety of other reasons.

These studies confirmed that the methods utilized by the CPS to extract accusations from children are guaranteed to contaminate the testimony. In conclusion, Ceci et al. warned,

> Therefore, it is of the utmost importance to examine the conditions relevant at the time of a child's original report about a criminal event in order to judge the suitability of using that child as a witness in the court. It seems particularly important to know the circumstances under which the initial report of concern was made, how many times the child was questioned, the questions the child was asked, the consistency of the child's report over a period of time. If the child's disclosure was made in a non-threatening, non-suggestible atmosphere, if the disclosure was not made after repeated interviews, if the adults who had access to the child prior to her testimony are not motivated to distort the child's recollections through relentless and potent suggestions and outright coaching, if the child's original report remains highly consistent over a period of time, then the young child would be judged to be capable of providing much that is forensically relevant. Absence of any of these conditions . . . ought to raise cautions in the mind of the court.[5]

Unfortunately, these favorable, nonpersuasive conditions do not generally exist when children are interrogated regarding abuse. At best, the questioners approach the child with a preconceived opinion of guilt, even if the child denies all wrongdoing on the part of the adult, questioning may persist for months or even years until the child is browbeaten into making an accusation. Questioners *always* ask leading questions, and there is seldom anyone present to represent the accused or even monitor the actions of the examiner. The test regarding Sam Stone involved two minutes of questioning for ten weeks, and the children proved highly susceptible to leading questions. But, this is nothing compared to the months of two-, three- and four-hour interrogations that young children are forced to endure for weeks, months, and in some cases years—conducted by highly paid, biased therapists.

A Case in Point

M. Kelly Michaels, a twenty-six-year-old nursery school teacher, was accused and convicted of 115 counts of child sexual abuse against twenty three- to five-year-old children in the Wee Care Nursery School. Sentenced to forty-seven years in prison, Kelly is appealing on grounds that "most of the children were subjected to relentless and single-minded interviews that were suggestive and even threatening."[6] While this book does not attempt to try the case or to determine the guilt or innocence of the accused, this case illustrates the abusive lengths to which CPS will go to illicit accusations.

The case against Kelly Michaels began when a four-year-old former student was having his temperature taken rectally by a nurse. The child said, "'That's what my teacher does to me at school.' When asked to explain, he replied, 'Her takes my temperature.'" Two days later, the child was questioned by an assistant prosecutor with the use of "anatomical" dolls. During the interview, the child proceeded to take the doll's temperature, and the case against Kelly was born.

A social worker was called in to meet with his parents. She promptly informed them that sexual abuse of children was epidemic, quoting the inaccurate statistic that one out of every three children is sexually abused, making it clear that their children were probably victims. She encouraged them to interpret any sign of genital soreness, bedwetting, changes in behavior, and nightmares as evidence that they had been mistreated.[7]

Police officers and social workers joined in the interrogations. Most of the children were told at the beginning of the interviews that their classmates had already said "that Kelly Michaels was a bad person who had hurt them." They were then encouraged to confirm stories of abuse. After all, would their friends lie?[8] This atmosphere of accusation was accompanied with rewards if the child complied and threats if the child denied any memory of abuse. For example, when Child 5C was questioned, the social worker said, "Do you want to sit on my lap? Come here. I am so proud of you. I love big girls like you that tell me what happened—that aren't afraid because I am here to protect you. . . . You got such pretty eyes. . . . I'm jealous, I'm too old for you."[9] (It's amazing that social workers can make statements about being too old for a child—if a lay person said that, he would be labeled a molester.)

The abusive tone of some interviews in this case is illustrated in the interview of Child 8C, conducted by a social worker, Mr. Fonolleras, and a police detective, Mastrangelo. (This interview is taken from an appellate court brief.)

> F: Don't be so unfriendly. I thought we were buddies last time.
>
> 8c: Nope, not any more.
>
> F: We have gotten a lot of other kids to help us since I last saw you. . . . Did we tell you that Kelly is in jail?
>
> 8c: Yes. My mother already told me.
>
> F: Did I tell you that this is the guy that arrested her? . . . Well, we can get out of here real quick if you just tell me what you told me last time, when we met.

8c: I forgot.

F: No you didn't. I know you didn't.

8c: I did! I did!

F: I thought we were friends last time.

8c: I'm not your friend any more.

F: How come?

8c: Because I hate you!

F: You have no reason to hate me. We were buddies when you left.

8c: I hate you now!

F: Oh, you do not, you secretly like me, I can tell.

8c: I hate you.

F: Oh come on. We talked to a few more of your
buddies. And everyone told me about the nap
room, and the bathroom stuff, and the music room
stuff, and the choir stuff, and the peanut butter
stuff, and everything. . . . All your buddies [talked].
. . . Come on, do you want to help us out? Do you
want to keep her in jail? I'll let you hear your voice
and play with the tape recorder; I need your help
again. Come on. . . . Real quick, will you just tell
me what happened with the wooden spoon? Let's
go.

8c: I forgot.

M: [the police officer] Now listen, you have to
behave.

F: Do you want me to tell him to behave? *Are you
going to be a good boy, huh?* [Emphasis added] While
you were here, did he [Det. Mastrangelo] *show you
his badge and handcuffs?* . . . [Emphasis added] Back
to what happened to you with the wooden spoon.
If you don't remember words, maybe you can show
me [with anatomical doll].

8c: I forgot what happened, too.

F: You remember. You told your mommy about everything, about the music room and the nap room, and all that stuff. You want to help her stay in jail, don't you? So she doesn't bother you anymore and so she doesn't tell you any more scary stories?[10]

This interview was typical of those conducted to gather "evidence" against Michaels, "with highly suggestive use of props and a relentless pursuit of only one hypothesis, often accompanied by bribes for disclosures and implied threats in the face of nondisclosure."[11] As a result of these interrogations, Michaels was charged with such bizarre acts as licking peanut butter off children's genitals, playing the piano in the music room while nude, making children drink her urine and eat her feces, and raping and assaulting them with knives, forks, spoons, and lego blocks. She allegedly did all of this over a seven month period, during the day in a busy day care center with numerous teachers and other adults walking in and out of her classroom and the music room. Not one single co-worker or parent ever witnessed her purported nudity or molestations. During the time Michaels had taught at the day care center, none of the children had complained to their parents, exhibited any abnormal behavior, or shown any anal, vaginal, or genital soreness or injury.[12] It seems somewhat suspicious that a fork, spoon, or knife could be inserted into a young child without injury or that kids would willingly attend school without complaint when they were being fed urine and feces. Most kids complain about vegetables. Yet, she was convicted on the basis of the interviews two and one-half years *after* these crimes were allegedly committed against very small children.

Common Practice

The elements of intimidation, threats, rewards, and repeated questioning are not unique to the Michaels' case; they are standard fare in the world of child protection. Abuse therapy has become a profitable industry, funded by tax dollars and fed by the child protective agencies. Therapists, convinced that any allegation is true, will often go to incredible lengths to extract confessions and then insist upon their validity in spite of the facts.

In Arizona, CPS took a young girl from home because of suspicion of sexual abuse. Although charges were dropped, the child remained in CPS custody. The couple separated, under CPS orders, so that the mother could get more visitation, but the promised visits have seldom materialized. Several years passed, and the child was under constant "therapy." At the age of thirteen, she began accusing the mother, several cousins, and the grandfather of molesting her. When the father learned of the recent charges, he called the caseworker to inquire when the grandfather had supposedly committed these acts. "The worker replied 'in 1986.' The father said, 'That is really strange because he died in 1982.' The caseworker said, 'There you go, calling her a liar again.'"[13] How does a person fight logic like that!

Interrogators seem to have little respect for the child. In one taped interview, a social worker insisted that a young boy accuse his father of abuse. However, the child insisted his father was innocent. After a while, the boy told the social worker he needed to use the bathroom. His request was ignored, and the relentless questions continued. As time went on, the boy continued to plead to be allowed to relieve himself, yet his distress was ignored. In time, the child became so desperate he was willing to say anything the social worker wanted, just so he could use the bathroom. The father was convicted and sentenced on the basis of a testimony extracted under torture.

There is a therapist in Colorado who has a reputation of "always getting her man." Armed with a master's degree in art, she never fails to conclude that molestation has occurred. In one incident, she was asked to evaluate two sisters, ages four and six years, respectively, regarding molestation by their father that supposedly occurred two years previously. The children had never confirmed the charges, and several psychiatrists (who are obviously more qualified than an art major) interviewed the children and stated that nothing improper had occurred. In a final effort to pursue the case, social workers brought the children in for another "evaluation" by this "therapist." After several sessions, a taped interview was made, which was used at the trial. On tape, the oldest child admitted crawling into bed with her parents one morning and touching her father on the penis. She also stated that her mother had told her that this was improper. (Considering the child was a curious four-year-old at the time, such an occurrence is not unlikely.) But, according to the child, nothing else transpired.

The "therapist" then handed the girls, one at a time, naked anatomical dolls. The youngest was bored with the whole process and wandered around looking for playthings. When she interviewed the oldest daughter, she handed her the doll face up and said, "Tell me where he let you pretend to shave him." The little girl turned the doll over and rubbed the back. The therapist responded, "No!" and turned the doll over again, face side up. She repeated her request, and the girl turned the doll over again and rubbed it on the back. This went on for an extended period of time, but the child never changed her response.

When the video was presented in court, the therapist told the jury that the child was nervous in front of the camera [she looked bored, not nervous] and that she had made other accusations in the past that were not taped. Based upon this hearsay evidence, the father, who still maintains his innocence, was found guilty and sentenced to an extended prison term.

Anatomical Dolls

A favorite tool in sex abuse interrogations are anatomically correct dolls. These dolls are made by a handful of companies throughout the country such as Gifford Products, a cottage industry founded by a Fruita couple.[14] Female dolls come equipped with a vagina, breasts, and pubic hair; their male counterpart has an exaggerated

penis, scrotum, and testicles. The dolls are used by therapists and social workers to facilitate findings of sexual
abuse. No controlled studies support the use of these
dolls, yet recent surveys indicate they are being used by
90 percent of the field professionals.[15]

One justification for this is that they allow children to
manipulate objects that will help them to recall a traumatic event, but that belief is based upon an assumption
of guilt. Children know dolls are objects, not real people,
and curious children will naturally explore the dolls, pulling
on anything sticking out and poking things into the holes.
Another problem is that the dolls are not used in a ster-
ile, nonsuggestive setting. Often they are only used after
children have been given detailed information about sexual
activities that may have occurred. This could influence
them in their interactions with the dolls. Studies indicate
that the child may behave sexually with the dolls, not
because of a history of abuse, but because of sexual discussions prior to their use.

Transcripts of therapy sessions involving the dolls
reveal the extreme bias on the part of the therapists.
Some of the practices used include "naming the dolls
after defendants, berating the dolls for alleged abuses
against the children, assuming the role of fantasy characters in doll play, and creating a persistent atmosphere of
accusation."[16]

Studies in which children who had never been abused
were allowed to play with these dolls, revealed that children naturally check out every hole and attachment. But,
just one session with the suggestive dolls did heighten
sexual awareness among the children, and their parents
reported a greater number of questions regarding the
child's sexuality.

In spite of the widespread use of these ugly atrocities,
many professionals and psychiatrists feel they should be
banned. Concerns are raised that they are suggestive and
encourage children to engage in sexual play even if they
have never been abused. Also, children may interact with
them in a "suggestive" manner out of curiosity. A child

may stick a finger in the holes just because they are there. Children naturally explore everything. No standardized tests have ever been run to assess doll play for non-abused children, and thereby establish a norm. Testimony based on anatomical dolls is so highly suspect that a few jurisdictions have banned them until scientific data is available.[17] Yet, children are being ripped from their homes, couples ordered to separate, and innocent people are being sent to prison on the sole basis of how a child plays with a doll.

Beyond Logic

The lengths to which some social workers and therapists will go to prove that abuse has occurred are amazing. Any fact can be twisted to support a guilty finding. If children play with the sexual organs and holes on the dolls, it is because they have been abused. If they avoid the private areas of the dolls or show embarrassment, it is because they are feeling guilty or embarrassed because they have been abused. If children are calm during vaginal exams, it is because they have been abused and have become desensitized to the touching of their genitals. If they struggle and resist the genital exam or become upset by the intrusion, the child's reluctance is blamed on traumatic sexual abuse. It's a no win situation; there is no provision for innocence.[18]

Another method used to drum up accusations is "disclosure therapy." For example, if a child colors with black or red, he may have been abused. If his scribbles contain elongated shapes, these are interpreted by therapists as phallic symbols. Any picture drawn by a child can be interpreted to support the bias of the "expert." In one case, a girl suspected of being an abuse victim, drew a picture of her father, her sister, and herself. They were all standing, smiles on their faces, with their hands upraised. When asked what the picture meant, she replied that it was a picture of her family cheering at a ballgame. However, the therapist testified that the child was wrong and that the upstretched arms were cries for help and a sign that the child had been abused.[19]

The damage that this tampered testimony has wreaked on American families is immeasurable. If the abusive tactics practiced on children to extract accusations were used on adults, the testimony would be thrown out of court. That same standard should apply to therapists and social workers who view themselves as "above the law."

Chapter Nine

Un*due* *Process*

Child Protective Services tramples the rights of both the accused and the victims it claims to protect. Operating behind a cloak of secrecy, child-savers commit perjury, defy court orders, and make a mockery of constitutional rights. Yet, this travesty continues almost unchallenged. Spurred by good intentions, we have created a malignant organism that is eroding the freedom and fabric of America's fundamental institution, the family.

Justice Louis D. Brandeis once wrote: "The greatest dangers to liberty lurk in insidious encroachment by men of zeal, well-meaning but without understanding." This echoes a sentiment shared by our Founding Fathers who enumerated within the Constitution individual rights that the government was not allowed to violate. These included, among others, the right to due process; freedom from self-incrimination; protection against illegal search and seizure; freedom of press, speech, and faith; and the right to a fair and speedy trial.

In their zeal to save battered children, well-meaning legislators have created a system described by a San Diego grand jury as "out of control, with few checks and with little balance."[1] Justice Tom Clark of Texas, a former U. S. attorney general, warns, "Nothing can destroy a government more quickly than its failure to observe its own laws, or worse . . . the charter of its own existence." The fact that workers in the child abuse industry violate constitutional rights daily is even recognized by some within the system. Philip Leduc, a CPS supervisor in

Northampton, Massachusetts, agreed that "if the level of intrusiveness perpetrated allegedly to protect children were attempted in any other field, we would be in court . . . we would be in jail, we would have the Supreme Court coming down with innumerable decisions against us."[2]

Presumption of Guilt

The cornerstone of American justice is the presumption that a person is innocent until proven guilty. This assumption, however, is reversed in the world of the child abuse industry. After losing a "mass molestation" case, prosecutor Kathleen Morris of Jordan, Minnesota, exclaimed that she was "sick to death of things like the presumption of innocence."[3] This is a sentiment shared by many workers within the child abuse industry. And, with leading "experts" claiming that abuse occurs in almost every American home, it's no wonder the system is out of balance.

Presumption of guilt is especially evident when the charge is sexual molestation—which makes this accusation such an effective weapon. Once again, the San Diego grand jury found that a mere suspicion to molest was sufficient to file a petition and to sustain a true finding. They wrote: "*The burden of proof, contrary to every other area of our judicial system, is on the alleged perpetrator to prove his innocence* [Emphasis theirs]."[4]

In spite of the numerous studies that prove that 60 to 80 percent of all abuse charges—including sexual abuse—are false, those within the industry still claim that any charge, no matter how ridiculous, is true. In their training literature, social workers are given "at risk" assessments for determining when abuse is likely. Jon Conte, in a manual titled *A Look at Child Abuse*, published by the National Committee for Prevention of Child Abuse (NCPCA), plays down the idea of "false" allegations of sexual abuse, claiming that they are extremely rare and only occur in cases of custody suits or divorce when an adult is manipulating a child. He assures that confessions made under the questioning of "skilled" social workers are all true. He does not acknowledge the extreme bias against parents, nor does he account for the coercion that takes place during "questioning" (see chapter 8). Instead, he insists that this hysteria stirred up regarding false claims is based on reluctance by adults to believe that something as evil as sexual abuse against children exists and our feelings of guilt and helplessness for not protecting children.

Mr. Conte then defines sexually abusive behavior in such a broad way that most parents could be considered guilty. For example, a parent who has watched a child dress or going to the bathroom is an abuser. Unfortunately, he does not even give any age guidelines here. How does a child learn to dress or get potty trained if a parent isn't watching and assisting? And, why does the presence of a parent always imply something sexual? Other "guilty" activities include kissing on the mouth, rubbing a child's back or head, or bathing a child if the adult has "sexual intent." It is left to the poorly trained, biased social worker, who was not present during the incident, to determine if the "intent" of the contact was abusive.

Once a complaint has been filed, it is often the responsibility of the caseworker to prove the claim. In fact, in an interdepartment memorandum from the Washington State Social Services Office, it even makes this duty part of their program directive.

I. Defining the Program

A. The Child Protective Services program should be oriented around *assessment of risk* of child maltreatment rather than substantiation of specific allegations of child abuse/neglect. *Investigation* of specific alleged instances of child abuse/neglect, *and findings* related to such investigations, *should be viewed as a means of strengthening and supporting risk assessment* [Emphasis added].[5]

Note: There is no mention here of ascertaining truth,

just of proving the caseworker's own preconceived no-
tion about risk. Risk assessments are as arbitrary as the
whims of the individual caseworker. Douglas Besharov,
former director of the National Center on Child Abuse
and Neglect (NCCAN) expressed concern at a 1992 convention that many states require all reports to be treated
as true, that those charged are to be presumed guilty.
This is the same totalitarian mindset employed during
the Spanish Inquisition, Hitler's reign, and Stalin's purges.

Central Registry

As the Nazi regime gained power, all citizens suspected of having Jewish ancestry were registered as en-
emies of the state. Those on such lists were required to
wear armbands and were prohibited from participation
in numerous activities. The child abuse industry maintains similar lists. Most states now maintain a Central
Registry of persons who are supposedly substantiated child
abusers. In reality, many states place the names of *everyone* accused of abuse on the registry. If the caseworker
eventually decides the case is unsubstantiated, then she
may have the name dropped.

If a person is found innocent of all charges in a
criminal court, their name is still kept on the registry as
a *confirmed* abuser. When questioned about the fairness
of this, one Central Registry director justified the practice
because social services uses a "different standard" to
determine guilt. Criminal courts require guilt beyond a
reasonable doubt; social services, on the other hand, only
requires "some credible evidence."[6] In the eyes of CPS,
an anonymous report is often considered "credible evidence," even if it came from a vindictive ex-spouse, neighbor, employee, tenant, etc.

Some states, such as Colorado, do have a process
whereby the accused may request a hearing to have their
name removed, but the success ratio is very low. Irwin
Zook was accused of molesting a foster child, even though
the child claimed that nothing improper had ever oc-

curred. Zook was never convicted of abuse, so he appealed to have his name removed from the Central Registry. Yet, Social Services refused to cooperate. "At one point during the 15-hour hearing a social worker was asked why she insisted the molestation took place when the youth denied it. 'Body language,' she replied, 'of the boy's testimony.'"[7] The hearing officer agreed to have Zook's name removed, but the state appealed the decision. They simply do not want to remove any name, innocent or not. In fact, notices were sent to new "perpetrators" on the registry informing them that "it is probable that your name will not be removed" if there is "credible evidence" for the alleged abuse.

In Massachusetts, accused parties who are being declared "substantiated" and listed in the registry receive a form letter from the Department of Social Services, which includes the following justification for the decision: "At least one person said you were responsible for the incident, and there was no available information to *definitely indicate otherwise.*"[8]

Attorney David Hofer says of the system, "It's really very shocking. They've turned the legal system upside down and stood it on its head. They should have to hold a hearing to get the name *on* the list. It's a violation of rights to have to prove your innocence."[9] Central Registry director, Jan Beveridge, feels it would change the philosophy behind CPS to only list names of convicted abusers. (That is precisely what is needed!) Besides, what's the big deal? After all, Beveridge said, "A criminal conviction could mean jail, but the registry is merely a list."[10]

However, this "mere" list is unconstitutional, and it carries with it a lifelong stigma. Anyone on the list is the first to be questioned when someone in the neighborhood is abused. People can be banned from their professions because they are on a list, even if they have been found innocent. People have been denied the right to adopt, to teach, or to work with children because an unfounded, anonymous tip placed their name on a registry of supposedly "confirmed" abusers.

In Colorado, *victims* of child abuse are listed as possible, future perpetrators until they turn twenty-eight—thus making the victim suffer again for the crime of another. This is done on the basis of the "cycle theory," that anyone who is abused will be an abuser. While it is logical that children learn to imitate behavior, it is just as logical for a person to grow up determined to treat children better than he was treated. Does every woman who has been raped become a rapist? Do people who have been robbed automatically become thieves? It is insulting to assume that human beings are mere animals programmed by their environment, totally incapable of self-determination.

The surveys that form the basis for the cycle theory were taken strictly from convicted abusers. When asked if they had ever been abused as a child, a large percentage agreed. However, in true CPS fashion, no control study was done. Since that time, surveys taken of control groups of people never charged with abuse prove that many abused children do grow up nonabusive.

Also listed on the registry are the names of children who reportedly have abused other children. If a child bruises a sibling, he may carry a lifetime stigma that will determine if he can adopt a child or work in certain careers. One mother received a notice that her toddler was listed on the state registry as a "confirmed sexual molester," because he had attempted to check out his baby sister's orifices with a color crayon. When the mother took the baby in to confirm that there was no injury, a report was sent in on the curious sibling, and he was branded as a pervert—years before he even knew the meaning of sex!

There is a growing push to set up a national registry. This would be a horrendous weapon to place in the hands of anyone with any reason, political or personal, to destroy the life and career of someone else.

Illegal Search and Seizure

The Fourth Amendment to the Constitution assures that "the right of the people to be secure in their persons, houses, papers and effects, against unreasonable searches and seizures, shall not be violated, and no Warrants shall issue, but upon probable cause." Unfortunately, most child-savers believe that they are exempt from this restriction. When a social worker arrives at the door, often accompanied by a police officer, they expect to be allowed to enter. Some CPS workers even insist that they do not need warrants. A Denver paper once stated that in Colorado, all that is needed to enter and search a home is "a belief" that a child *may* be abused. That belief can be based upon one anonymous phone call.

Because this is intimidating, most people allow social workers to enter—especially if they are innocent of any charge. Surely, they assume, the social worker will see what a ridiculous charge this is, and the case will be settled. However, that is the biggest mistake an innocent person can make. Once people have allowed an agent in their home, they have actually waived their Fourth Amendment rights. Since most social workers believe that the accused is already guilty, they often go into a home, fishing for reasons to draw the family into the system. Many innocent families have been drawn into the nightmare of CPS because they allowed a social worker in the house—only to have the children removed because of dirty dishes in the sink and laundry on the floor.

Once in the home, social workers often insist that they be allowed to strip search the children and interview them alone. This is a damaging, traumatic experience for a child, tantamount to molestation. No child should be forced to stand naked before the probing eyes and hands of a stranger. Children are taken aside and questioned without witnesses. They ask things such as "How often do your parents spank you? Have your parents ever touched you in a private area? How do they do it? Have you ever taken a shower with a parent? Have your parents ever slept with you?" No matter how innocent the answers, a social worker on a mission can always find a reason to remove a child if they desire. After all, the child could be in denial. Because these interviews usually take place without a parent present, the child's words can be twisted to mean whatever the caseworker wishes them to mean.

If a parent refuses, the social worker immediately demands to know what evil the family is attempting to hide. They counter with threats to get a warrant, remove the child, and throw the parents in jail; but parents should stand up for their rights. Children do not have to be questioned in your home, nor does *anyone* have the right to enter your home without a warrant issued by a court; and getting a warrant requires probable cause, not mere suspicion.

This is a tactic that is being used regularly against home school families. There are an estimated one million children in America who are now being educated at home, a fact that irritates the National Education Association (NEA). Of these families, 85 to 90 percent identify them- selves as Christians and have made this educational choice one of religious convictions as well as a desire to provide an education for their children that is superior to what is offered by our failing public schools.[11] Home schooled children typically place *at* or *above* the eightieth percentile in achievement tests, which means they are in the top 20 percent of the nation.

Obviously, this is an option that works. Perhaps that is one reason that the academic community opposes the movement. Many teachers, like social workers, believe that parents check their brains at the door of the mater- nity ward. They are convinced that they, not the parents, have the right to determine what a child needs—that parents are typically selfish or too stupid to put the child's needs above their own. Educators have failed to shut the home school movement down through the courts, so they are turning to CPS for assistance. There they have found willing allies.

Social workers are typically suspicious of parents anyway, and, as one caseworker said, "Pulling a child out to home school is seen as a red flag. What is the parent trying to hide?" Christopher Klicka, senior counsel for the Home School Legal Defense Association (HSLDA), confirms this trend.

> I have handled thousands of legal conflicts in the last seven years between home schoolers and the state, and this year there have been more child welfare and social service investigations than all of the previous years combined. I used to talk to a child welfare agent every other month, but now I talk to at least two agents per week.[12]

Klicka has traced many of these abuse complaints to school principals and truant officers, who see CPS as a "back door" to shutting down home schools.

The Home School Legal Defense Association (HSLDA) is an organization set up to provide legal assistance for members against such encroachments. While some home school parents who do not belong to HSLDA have had children removed, no member family of HSLDA has ever lost a child to the system or been forced to stop home schooling. The attorneys for HSLDA advise parents to *never* allow social workers or police officers into their homes without a warrant. Though social workers often threaten to come back with warrants, this rarely happens.

If a social worker or truant officer comes to the home of a HSLDA member, they are refused entrance, however the family does take steps to assure the workers that the children are safe. First, they call an attorney at HSLDA and hand the phone out the door to the agent. Often, the attorney can satisfy the caseworker. If more evidence is needed, the family will take their children to their own doctor, who submits a report to the social worker regarding their well-being. Also, character witnesses can submit statements. In most cases this is sufficient.

From his experience, Chris Klicka concludes that many social workers do not understand constitutional rights or due process. (So much for public education!) He tells of one instance when a caseworker insisted that there was no such thing as a Fourth Amendment right against illegal search and seizure. Another social worker was shocked when Klicka refused to allow a member's children to be subjected to the humiliation of a strip search. "No one else ever refused a strip search before," she charged and went on to imply that the family had something to hide. But, in each case, the family that exerted its rights won.[13]

There was a case in Alabama, however, which HSLDA actually took to the state court of appeals. A low-income, home school mother was turned in anonymously for possible child abuse and educational neglect by a woman who admitted that she did not personally know the family or their situation. When a caseworker arrived, demanding to examine the home and interrogate the children, the family refused under Klicka's counsel. A report from the children's doctor confirming their well-being, as well as statements from neighbors who knew the family, were submitted to the caseworker who stated that she personally believed the children were all right. However, the department was not satisfied. Possibly afraid that this might set a precedent, Human Resources filed abuse charges and had a hearing before a lower court to decide if an anonymous tip was cause enough to allow the social worker to enter the home and question the children. The lower court agreed that any reports of abuse, even anonymous reports, were sufficient to establish "cause shown," and demanded that the family comply or be charged with contempt of court.

Michael Farris, attorney and president of HSLDA, immediately filed an appeal with the court of appeals on the basis of the Fourth Amendment requirement of "probable cause," and requested a stay of the search warrant. The stay was granted, and, on 28 August 1992, the Alabama Court of Civil Appeals reversed the lower court decision. Setting a significant precedent, the court ruled that an anonymous tip was not sufficient to show "probable cause" and to allow CPS to search a home. Klicka states, "To our knowledge, this is the first appellate court case that significantly curtails the powers of the social service agents." The court properly ruled that:

> The "cause shown" [in this case] was unsworn hearsay and could, at best, present a mere suspicion. A mere suspicion is not sufficient to rise to reasonable cause or probable cause.[14]

Due Process

Embodied in the Fifth, Sixth, and Fourteenth Amendments of the Constitution are the rights of due process—the right of a fair trial. Through subsequent litigation, the rights of due process have come to mean the following:

The right to receive notice of all charges.

The right to counsel.

The right to confront your accuser and to cross-examination of the complainants.

The right to exercise a privilege against self-incrimination.

The right to a transcript of all proceedings.

The right to appellate review.

The right to subpoena witnesses and subpoena documentary evidence to support your position or contradict evidence presented against you.

The right to a trial by jury.

The right to receive equal protection of the law.

The right to use the Constitution as a defense.

The right to use case law as a defense.

The right to sue any U. S. citizen for "Unlawful Deprivation of any constitutional, statutory, or administrative right."

The right of access and use of any taxpayer-funded law-library, government building, and courtroom.

The protection against double jeopardy.

The Child Protection System does not recognize any of these elements of due process. It has become a police state within the state, operating outside the bounds of the Constitution.

The Curtain of Confidentiality

CPS uses a "curtain of confidentiality" as justification for denying due process. After all, they explain, they are simply in the business of saving children, and the end justifies the means. After the allegations of gross misconduct in the Wade case were made public through the local press, a San Diego grand jury convened a massive investigation of the local Social Services Department. While many people outside the department were willing to assist the grand jury, Social Services was not. Their attempts to observe the system in action "were blocked" by DSS and County Counsel with the explanation that the jury's observations would be violating the confidentiality of their clients.[15]

The jury concluded, "This lack of cooperation with the grand jury exemplifies the mind-set in which DSS operates. Closed courtrooms, confidential files, and total statutory immunity create an attitude unbecoming an agency purportedly serving the best interests of the community." DSS further cautioned that complaints about the system came from unreliable "fringe" groups who wished to weaken Social Services' powers and allow more children to die.[16]

The grand jury investigation began at the request of a local congressman. Within a short time the grand jury received almost fifty complaints about the Juvenile Dependency System. After the media exposure on the Wades' case, the jury was flooded with an additional two hundred cases. Social Services repeatedly attempted to reassure the jury that the newspaper articles were filled with distortions in the Wade case. If it weren't for confidentiality laws, representatives from Social Services and the police department assured the jury, it would be apparent that the news coverage was grossly distorted.

As a result, the Grand Jury subpoenaed from DSS, County Counsel, The Center for Child Protection, Children's Hospital, the District Attorney, the San Diego Police Department, Naval Investigative Services, NAVCARE, Voices for Children, and individual professionals, all documents relating to the criminal prosecution of Albert Carder. Review of these documents and sworn testimony before the jury only confirmed our view that this was a case which never should have been in the Juvenile system. It also confirmed the overall accuracy of the *San Diego Union* in this case.[17]

Investigation of all the cases before them brought the jury to the conclusion that there were three hundred cases in their county alone that had elements of the Wade case and proved massive abuse perpetrated by DSS. Regarding the curtain of confidentiality, the jury argues, "confidentiality in the juvenile system can be used, not for the best interest of the child, but as both sword and shield against the families and the public."[18]

The Faceless Witness

Under the guise of "confidentiality," CPS allows anonymous complaints as cause for investigation and evidence for conviction. On the basis of anonymous tips, houses are illegally searched, parents arrested, children abducted from their homes and schools, and families thrown into emotional and financial ruin. People can be sent to prison on child abuse charges without ever being allowed to cross-examine their accusers.

Claiming that children are traumatized by testifying, therapists are quick to ban children from the court room. Often kids will be in therapy for months while therapists attempt to manipulate them into accusing their parents. Once the child has been coaxed, they attempt to videotape the session. When videos are not used, or when the child does not make a "proper accusation," therapists are allowed to testify that the child has made an accusation, and their unsubstantiated testimony is accepted as fact. This is particularly damaging to the accused because there is no testimony regarding the setting under which any accusation was made and the level of coercion involved. Nor is the accused allowed the opportunity to cross-examine testimony against him. This is clearly a violation of the United States Constitution.

In some cases, therapists, attorneys, and caseworkers have been known to lie under oath regarding the nature of the accusations. In a hearing in St. Louis, Missouri, Judge John Chancellor found Assistant Circuit Attorney Jan Geiler guilty of concealing evidence. Geiler repeatedly told the grand jury that the attempt to video the alleged victim was unsuccessful, concealing the fate that the video did indeed exist. A report on the incident stated,

> As it turned out, to them "unsuccessful" meant the girl didn't make any accusations. There actually was a video tape, and the girl said she forgot what her mother told her to say![19]

Although the accused is guaranteed the right to see all the evidence against him in order to guarantee a fair trial, CPS repeatedly fails to comply. Parents continually complain about not being able to see transcripts or videos. Chris Klicka relates a conversation with a Christian social worker who is also a home school parent. The worker agreed that many social workers were very deceptive in sharing evidence. He stated that a person did have the right to request that his record be expunged if the allegation was proven to be unfounded. A parent *does* have the right to demand to see all of the evidence in his file, though the social worker will often refuse to comply on the grounds of "confidentiality." "'At that point,' he said 'the social worker is bluffing. If a person just evokes the Freedom of Information Act, the social worker is required by law to show him the records in the case file.'"[20]

Self-Incrimination

"No person shall be . . . compelled in any criminal case to be a witness against himself . . ." by the Fifth Amendment to the Constitution.

This amendment guarantees that no person who is being investigated or tried can be forced to confess or give testimony that might hurt himself or herself. A person has the right to remain silent, nor can the prosecution even mention that a person has exercised this right. Yet, this right is consistently violated by the child abuse industry. For example, when a person is accused of molestation, many states require that the person undergo a penile plethysmograph in conjunction with a polygraph, in spite of the fact that there is no scientific data validating these devices. The courts have consistently ruled that the results of a polygraph are only allowed under very rigid restrictions. No one can legally be forced to undergo such tests. Although parents will often comply with these requests in a frantic effort to get their children back. A therapist, who generally thinks the parent is guilty, will "interpret" the results and use them as a basis for making recommendations, which the court will generally follow.

This practice was challenged by a police officer, Norman Harrington, who was accused of being part of a large sex ring. No evidence could be found against Harrington, and he was never charged with a crime, yet he was fired from his job when he refused to submit to a penile plethysmograph, a test that he found offensive and degrading. In June 1993, after years of litigation, a federal jury found that Harrington's constitutional rights had been violated when he had been ordered to take the test. The city eventually settled with Harrington for nine hundred thousand dollars.[21]

The accused are often required to testify against themselves to therapists. When a family enters the system, they are routinely fed to department-approved therapists, but what occurs in these sessions is not confidential because therapists are mandated reporters. They seem to exist for the sole purpose of gathering evidence against the family. If parents refuse to confess, they are pegged as uncooperative, unrepentant, or in denial. If they express anger and frustration over the capture of their children and their treatment at the hands of CPS, they are labeled violent, manic depressive, or paranoid.

This practice was condemned by the San Diego Grand Jury.

> Psychological evaluations are ordered routinely. The evaluators are chosen on a rotating basis from a pool. Choice of a therapist is usually left to the discretion of the social worker. Not even lip service is paid to the need to find a therapist congenial to the client.
>
> The Jury recommends that, when therapy is ordered, the client should receive a selection of therapists from which to choose. . . . The therapist should certainly not be chosen by the DSS social worker responsible for prosecuting the case.
>
> *The jury is not convinced that all of these children and parents need therapists* [Emphasis theirs]. There is some concern that the inevitable court order for a therapist is feeding another sub-industry of the system.[22]

Triple Jeopardy

Another element of due process guaranteed by the Fifth Amendment is the no "person shall be subject for the same offense to be twice put in jeopardy . . ." clause. However, people accused of child abuse may actually be placed in jeopardy two, three, or even four times. Because civil and juvenile courts are outside the realm of the criminal justice system, they are not bound by this constraint. If criminal charges are brought against a person for child abuse, they are supposedly granted the rights of due process.

However, a determination of innocence in criminal court does not carry any weight in family court. Even if parents are declared not guilty, they can be stripped of all parental rights in juvenile court and lose their children permanently. This occurs because juvenile court requires a different level of proof. Where criminal courts demand proof "beyond a reasonable doubt," juvenile courts only require a "preponderance of evidence." It doesn't matter that the evidence is slanted, that the defendant is often not allowed to even view the evidence against himself, cross-examine witnesses, or require the victim to be examined by an expert of his own choice.

Professionals charged with abuse and listed in central registries may also be subjected to professional licensing hearings. Even though there may be no criminal conviction, doctors, teachers, day car providers, camp directors, counselors, pastors, and others who work with children or in a capacity of trust may find that their professional standing is jeopardized by the suspicion of guilt.

An accused abuser may also be subject to civil suits. While this seems only fair for those who have suffered abuse at the hand of others, it may also be a prime motivation behind the onslaught of "False Memory" claims being launched. During therapy, people going to counseling for depression, addictions, or eating disorders are suddenly recalling "hidden memories" of sexual abuse suffered at the hands of their parents. They are told by therapists that they can only be healed from the damage of these hidden memories by cutting off all family ties, suing their parents for large sums of money, and, of course, continuing in counseling—all at a fee. Therapists are thereby guaranteed a continuing clientele, and attorneys who file the claims typically keep one-third of any money collected.

Although many people claim that these "hidden memories" are nothing more than suggestions planted by unscrupulous or misguided therapists, there is a similarity between the methods used by therapists who hunt for hidden memories. They all share a belief that sexual abuse is the cause of all psychological ills. They employ hypnosis, body massage, and imaging. Shirley Souza, a woman who was convicted with her husband of raping two granddaughters and accused of abusing her own daughters when they were children, said the daughter who accused her regained her "memories" through hypnosis and relaxation therapy. The other daughter denies any wrongdoing on the part of the parents.[23]

While some children do repress memories they feel are too traumatic to handle, the methods utilized by specialists in "hidden memories" are highly suspect. Family members who have been torn apart by such accusations consider "the network of counselors, psychotherapists, social workers, radical feminists and New Age self-help groups aimed at 'healing the inner child' and 'reparenting' as evil, cultish and bent on destroying traditional families."[24] Survivors of this abusive therapy who have retracted their accusations agree that they were led to believe they were sexually abused when, in fact, no abuse had ever occurred.

The Right to a Trial

What surprises many parents is that they can lose their children—the most important part of their lives—without ever having a trial. The Constitution does guarantee that no person shall be "deprived of life, liberty or property, without due process of law." But, child-savers reason that children are people, not property, so this clause does not apply to them. As usual, the child abuse industry is above the law. The Sixth Amendment further states that "in all criminal prosecutions, the accused shall enjoy the right to a speedy and public trial, by an impartial jury." Once again, the child abuse industry claims exemption because they are not part of the "criminal" system.

This situation leaves many parents in limbo. Presumed guilty, they are denied any chance to be with their families. When police departments refuse to pursue investigations of charges they believe to be groundless, social workers are reluctant to let go. These parents are in a state of legal limbo, sometimes for years, without ever having their day in court.

Leslie Perdian found himself in this situation. A disabled Vietnam War veteran, Perdian and his wife developed a small business selling electric parts to the city, local air force base, and to private businesses. Since both he and his wife worked, they hired a couple in their condo complex to baby-sit their eight-year-old daughter.

The situation was rocky from the start. The girl felt she was being mistreated. She also believed that the baby-sitters had pornographic videos. On 19 July the daughter called CPS to turn in the baby-sitters. An investigator came out and charged the father—not the baby-sitter—with molestation and carried her off to a foster home. The CPS worker simply took the girl and left, not even leaving a notice. When Jeanine Perdian arrived to pick up her daughter, no one knew where she was. The police finally located the girl.

According to CPS, the daughter accused her father on video. The girl has a different story, claiming that she repeatedly defended her father, but that they "wouldn't take 'no' for an answer, and 'coached her' to implicate her father on tape, saying 'when you're ready to tell the truth, we'll turn the tape back on.'" What actually appears on the tape is unknown. CPS refuses to allow the family and their attorney to view it.

The daughter could only return home if Leslie moved out of the home, which he did. Even though the girl moved back with her mother, CPS regained custody of her. No charges were filed against the father; the police believe the man is innocent, but he was never given an opportunity to clear his name. Instead of having a trial to determine guilt or innocence, Perdian was notified that a hearing would be held to request that legal custody go to the state and both parents be stripped of all parental rights. If the state were to win, the Perdians would never see their daughter again, even though they have never been charged with or convicted of a crime.[25]

Examining the Evidence

Therapists and social workers often forbid the alleged victim to appear in court. This is too traumatic, they say, and, in some cases, they may be right. But, too often, this is a tool to keep children from exonerating their parents. To replace the trauma of personal appearance, testimony is videotaped—but, even the videos are withheld from the accused. How could a videotape possibly be intimidated? This is a blatant violation of constitutional rights. These videos, when used in court, are an inadequate substitute for testimony because of the questionable way in which the testimony is extracted and the lack of an advocate for the defense actively involved in the questioning.

A classic example of this is the case of an Arizona teacher who had been labeled as a child molester by CPS. The teacher filed a suit claiming "that State officials violated his civil rights by denying him a hearing, libeled and slandered him and his family, wrongfully interfered with his employment, and caused him severe physical, emotional and economic damage."[26]

His suit was based in large part upon the evidence that CPS ignored and refused to admit. For example, the child who had been molested had never accused the teacher. The child had actually accused someone else, but, since he was a friend of the family, the accusation was ignored. In fact, the CPS agent stated that the child had fantasized the incident with the "friend of the family." That "friend" later pled guilty to child sexual molestation in a very similar case and was convicted. Then, the CPS worker denied ever knowing of the allegations against the "friend." During police investigations, the child denied that the teacher had ever molested him. The police supposedly communicated this information to CPS, but the caseworker denied any knowledge of the child's testimony.

In spite of the gross mishandling of this affair, the teacher's suit was denied. The court claimed that CPS workers were immune from civil prosecution for their activities.[27]

Just Compensation

An important element for creating balance in the legal system is the right of a person slandered or otherwise wrongly accused to seek redress for damages. But, this right is denied everyone who is falsely charged with child abuse. Limited immunity is necessary to protect law enforcement agents who, in good faith, must be free to investigate criminal charges. However, when the charge is child abuse, the broad immunity granted to all "good faith" reporters has been stretched to protect caseworkers who lie under oath, therapists who are guilty of gross malpractice, and sloppy investigative techniques. It has removed all accountability from the system, creating a system that reeks of corruption and tramples the rights of the innocent.

In an interview with the author, a Christian social worker, who is also a parent, was asked how she would respond if a social worker appeared at her door. She replied, "I wouldn't let him in. Then my husband and I would abandon everything we have and leave that night." That's quite an indictment from a person who has seen the system from the inside.

Chapter Ten

A Trial by Jury

The Sixth Amendment of the Constitution guarantees the right of the accused to a trial by an *impartial* jury of peers; but when the charge is an emotional issue such as child molestation, impartiality is difficult to achieve, and the obvious bias of many judges creates an imbalance in presenting the case. Prosecutors are granted great latitude in using hearsay evidence and suppressing testimony that might exonerate the accused. The defendant is often denied the right to call his own witnesses, to bring forth evidence to impeach his accusers, or to even examine the evidence against him. With such an unbalanced presentation, even the best meaning jury would have difficulty reaching an impartial verdict.

But, some judges, prosecutors, and even fellow jurors actually intimidate jury members. One judge was kicked off the bench by the California Supreme Court for repeatedly violating defendant's constitutional rights. "During one trial, Judge McCullough had actually instructed the jury, 'Ladies and gentlemen, I want you to go into that room and find the defendant guilty.'"

Combined with a natural fear of turning a molester loose to prey on more children, this intimidation creates an incredible pressure on juries to reach a guilty verdict. The whole premise of our justice system is reversed in molestation cases as juries are told it's better to send an innocent man to prison than to take the chance of letting the guilty go free. A classic example of this problem occurred in 1993 in a small Colorado community.

Dwayne and Cindy were married after a brief courtship. It didn't take long, Dwayne says, before he discovered how little he knew about his new wife. For example, she was older than he had thought. He also discovered that he was her fourth husband, something not previously disclosed.

The marriage was stormy from the beginning. The children were used to doing as they pleased, and they seldom attended school. After Dwayne became part of the family, he attempted to instill a measure of discipline in the home, something that was deeply resented by the kids. When the twelve-year-old daughter began dating boys sixteen-years-old and older, Dwayne objected. The girl looked more mature than she was, and he was concerned for her safety, knowing that she lacked the experience and sophistication to deal with the dating pressures older boys could exert. Unaccustomed to any authority, the daughter rebelled.

Eventually, Dwayne became convinced that the relationship was beyond repair and moved out of the home for good. A short time later, he was stunned to learn that the twelve-year-old and her mother had filed a molest charge against him. The nightmare had begun.

As Dwayne and his family began to prepare for his defense, he discovered that similar charges had been launched against the other husbands. One husband, who had left with another married woman, was anonymously turned in for suspicion of molesting the new girlfriend's children—charges that were eventually dropped due to lack of evidence. Another husband was accused of raping the son. When located, the man—who is remarried and has children of his own—denied all wrongdoing. No formal charges were ever brought against him.

Yet another husband, who had moved to Arizona when the marriage ended, was accused of raping Cindy at knifepoint. Though the man had witnesses who verified his presence in Arizona at the time of the alleged rape, he was transported back to Colorado. There he spent six months in jail, without a trial, before the district attorney's office acknowledged that it was improbable that the man could have been in two states at the same time. While this evidence might indicate a bias on the part of the accusers, none of it was allowed in court.

Selecting the Evidence

The San Diego grand jury expressed concern that when a charge of molestation is made, the evidence is often slanted to prove guilt, and evidence that might exonerate the accused is often deliberately concealed. Dwayne Cardin reached the same conclusion. On 9 October 1992 the girl (N.) was taken to a physician for examination of possible abuse. The doctor noted that the child had suffered a broken labia in 1984 after falling off a counter and had a history of vaginal (mainly yeast) infections. In her report to police, Dr. Danahey stated, "The physical examination can neither rule in or out sexual penetration at this time." After recounting the girl's accusation that Dwayne had molested her on numerous occasions between 1988 and April 1992, the doctor concluded:

> My expert opinion is that N. has been sexually abused, and most likely by her step-father, Dwayne, as she states. I base this on the fact that she has had several vaginal infections, her somewhat depressed affect, and *the fact that Dwayne is a very jealous and controlling person* [Emphasis added].[1]

The report, which was given considerable weight in the trial, failed to include the following information:

> 1. The history of vaginal infections began in 1986, two years *before* Dwayne entered the scene, a fact that was well-documented in the child's medical records.

> 2. The accident which resulted in the broken labia occurred four years before Dwayne became a part of the family.

> 3. Many of the vaginal yeast infections occurred after a series of antibiotics, which is a very common side effect.

4. The primary reason for the "expert" conclusion that Dwayne was a molester was Dr. Danahey's assessment of his personality. Yet, Dr. Danahey, who is not a qualified psychologist, *had never even met or spoken with Dwayne Cardin.* Her "expert opinion" was based solely on the hearsay evidence of the young girl.

N. insisted that she had never had intercourse with anyone but Dwayne and that he had always forced himself on her. When Dwayne heard of the charges, he asked for a second medical opinion—a reasonable request for a man who was facing a possible forty-year prison term. The judge refused.

After news began to travel around the small community, a close friend of N. approached the investigating officers, concerned that Dwayne was being framed. She told of numerous conversations with N. in which N. had described in detail sexual encounters she had with two different boyfriends, who were sixteen and eighteen-years-old, respectively. Also, she confirmed that N. had been staying with her during part of the time when the assaults were supposedly occurring.

But, most importantly, she provided the police with a possible motive for false charges. In her statement, she told police that N. and her older brother C. would become angry when Dwayne would ground her for drinking, smoking, and staying out late. According to the friend, Dwayne tried to fill the role of a reasonable father, but N. would frequently disobey and defiantly engage in activities that Dwayne felt were inappropriate for someone who was not quite thirteen years old.

She claimed that C. and N. confided in her their desire to have their mother sent back to a mental institution and then kill Dwayne. According to her story, C. had said he planned to

> Get up in the middle of the night, [at] one or two in the morning and cut the brakes on Dwayne's car because he hated him and wanted to kill him. And he would plot murder's [sic] how he was going

to burn the trailer up and how they were gonna
do anything they can to get out of the house because they didn't like their mom and their dad
and they didn't want to live there anymore.[2]

The motive for this, she said, was because Dwayne
wouldn't let N. "get her way and . . . go cruise Main or
go out and party with her friends, smoke and stuff like
that."[3] C. and N. allegedly told this friend that if they
could get rid of Dwayne and their mom, they could live
with the grandparents where they felt free to do as they
pleased. On another occasion, N. was quoted as saying
that she thought she could move in with her boyfriend if
she could get rid of Dwayne.

Though this testimony was part of the police records
and could have vindicated the defendant, it was not given
any weight in the trial.

The Trial

When the case finally went to trial on 13 December
1993, it was immediately apparent to the defense counsel,
as well as to a number of people in the audience, that the
attitude in the court was clearly biased. Seventy-five percent of the objections made by the defense were over-
ruled; seventy-five percent of the objections made by the
prosecution were sustained.[4] A motion asking the judge
to disqualify herself (when the case was to be retried) was
accompanied by five sworn affidavits from people who
had observed the trial proceedings, testifying to apparent
bias. One man, who did not even know the defendant,
said "that at one point during the jury trial proceedings,
I felt moved to stand up in court and assert my opinion
as to the bias of the judge in favor of the prosecuting
attorney."[5]

These observers perceived the "judge's ruling on
objections presented by both the prosecuting attorney
and defense counsel to be slanted highly in favor of the
prosecuting attorney."[6] Some complained that the judge
was "strict and stern with the Defense Attorney while
maintaining a friendly and pleasant attitude toward the

District Attorney."[7] One affidavit noted that "Judge
Marshall cut off the defense attorney during discussions
or questioning of witnesses, refusing to allow him to recall
a witness, and showing obvious dislike for the defendant
and defense counsel in the presence of the jury."[8]

Other witnesses felt the judge acted "in an inatten-
tive, lackadaisical and otherwise bored manner towards
the defense attorney and the defendant."[9] One felt that
the judge appeared "to be frustrated, angry and to wrinkle
her forehead in disgust whenever she sustained one of
the Defense Attorney's objections."[10] When the defense
attorney addressed the bench, questioned witnesses, or
presented arguments, the judge was allegedly observed
"physically leaning back in her chair, looking away from
the defense attorney," yet, when the district attorney would
make her presentations, the judge was observed "to be
attentive, interested, smiling and physically sitting for-
ward in her chair."[11]

Other examples of the uneven handling of the defense and prosecution were listed in the Motion to Disqualify. These included:

> 9. At one point in the recent trial proceedings, the
> District Attorney was allowed to read verbatim from
> a prior statement when questioning her witness
> without action or intervention by the Judge, while
> Defense counsel was disallowed to proceed in a
> similar manner regarding the same issue with his
> witness.
>
> 10. Prior to the recent trial, defense counsel re-
> quested an additional medical examination of the
> alleged victim, but was denied his request as the
> Judge stated another examination might result in
> possible trauma to the alleged victim, and that
> defense counsel had failed to state a compelling
> reason for the additional examination.
>
> 11. Contrary to the Judge's ruling, the District At-
> torney proceeded to have a far more detailed and
> intrusive examination of the alleged victim con-
> ducted without reprimand by or sanctions from

the Court, despite the fact the District Attorney had not complied with the criteria explained to the Defense Attorney by the Court.[12]

A Question of Integrity

The second medical exam, involving more sophisticated equipment, was performed about one year after the last alleged molestation occurred and indicated that the girl was sexually active. There was no evidence, however, to show that the partner had been Dwayne, except N.'s testimony that she had never been sexually involved with anyone else. Dwayne's concern over N. dating boys much too old for her was portrayed as a lover's jealousy.

While on the stand, N. testified that Dwayne had fondled and molested her for years. Although she claimed that he was constantly telling her not to reveal the activities to her mother, she also stated that he had repeatedly asked her to have his child and threatened to artificially inseminate her if need be to accomplish this objective— a strange request for someone who was trying to keep his activities a secret! The inconsistency of this was lost on many jurors. In fact, it was this bizarre element of the testimony that helped confirm guilt in the minds of several jurors.

All of the alleged incidents were supposed to have occurred at night, in a small bedroom where the two sisters shared bunk beds, while the younger girl slept. When questioned, the sister denied all knowledge of any sexual activities, but this was discounted because the younger girl was supposedly going deaf and could not hear at night when she removed her hearing aids. Once again the testimony was inconsistent, since the young girl recalled hearing the door squeak at night when her parents would check on her.

[Atty:] You talked about you heard the door open. . . . you wear hearing aids, don't you?

[Child:] Yeah.

[Atty:] You have hearing problems. Do you sleep with your hearing aids on?

[Child:] No, I cannot.

[Atty:] OK, so if you had your hearing aid off, you could hear that door open?

[Child:] Cause it's really squeaky.

[Atty:] Oh, so without your hearing aid you can still hear things?

[Child:] Uh huh. I don't have em in right now.[13]

It seemed incomprehensible that a child who could hear the bedroom door squeak could sleep through numerous sessions of intercourse, complete with conversations in which the accused begged N. to have his child, and *never* wake up. Yet, the significance of this was also lost on most of the jury.

The entire case rested upon the testimony of one person, the alleged victim, and the fact that medical exams, taken a year after the molestation supposedly occurred, revealed that she was sexually active. The "victim" repeatedly denied any sexual contact with any other male, yet the defense was very suspicious. In preliminary hearings, N. had been slender and wearing a dress. Now she was wearing sweat pants—very unusual attire for her—and a blouse that might have been a maternity garment. The defense attorney expressed his concern that N., now fourteen-years-old, might be pregnant. Upon request, Dr. Danahey claimed to have performed a pregnancy test which came back negative.

Jury Intimidation

When the case went to the jury, a roll call vote was taken: the results were ten guilty, two not guilty. Conversations with jurors indicated that most of them were convinced of Dwayne's guilt before the trial had even commenced. This was based on a conviction that the police had investigated and would not have arrested the defendant if he had not been guilty. It was hard to believe that so many people could be wrong.

It didn't take long for the mood in the jury room to heat up. The two hold-outs were viciously attacked for their positions. A second vote was cast, and the ballots were eleven to one. The remaining juror, who admits that he also went into the trial somewhat biased against the accused, felt that guilt had not been proven beyond a reasonable doubt. He was concerned about the inconsistencies in the testimony and had serious reservations about N.'s credibility. The more hostile the others became, the more determined he was not to cave in and violate his conscience.

Somehow, in violation of state law, word slipped out of the jury room revealing the identity of the one member who was voting not guilty. Quickly the character assassination began. Rumors spread that the juror was a convicted child molester himself and had served time in prison for the offense. The rumors were so convincing that even the defense counsel wondered if it might be true, but it wasn't. The juror in question had just been granted a gambling license, a process that requires background checks by the FBI and state law enforcement officials. Gambling licenses are not granted to convicted felons.

Late that first evening, the jury informed the judge that they could not reach a verdict. She ordered them to return the next day and try again. Suddenly, the district attorney offered a plea bargain. If Dwayne would just plead guilty, then the sentence would be reduced from forty years to ninety days and probation. Though the stakes were high, Dwayne refused to give up his rights to appeal and plead guilty to a crime he did not commit.

The jury convened the second day and remained deadlocked. They asked the remaining juror if he would be willing to "agree to disagree" and just vote guilty, regardless of his personal opinions. The juror refused. Then, the viciousness returned. One woman reportedly told the hold-out that "I pray to God that he will give me strength to curse you everyday!" Others accused him of holding out so he could collect the juror fee—as if it paid enough to take that kind of abuse. It became so heated that people sitting in an adjoining room could hear the screaming. At one point, the juror left the group and went to sit alone in a second jury room. The other members visited him, one at a time, to try to convince him to change his mind. But, he stood firm in his convictions. If he had not done so, an innocent man would be in prison.

The jury was hung, and a mistrial declared. Once the trial was over, the one juror who had been convinced of Dwayne's innocence discovered the destructive rumors that had branded him a molester as well. He quickly set the record straight, but, just as quickly, word spread that the district attorney's office was going to launch a child molestation investigation against him. Since a new trial was set for January, the message was clear to everyone in the small community: vote "not guilty," and you may find yourself the object of similar charges.

Vindication

The defense filed a motion requesting that the judge step aside from the case, and the motion was denied. Because of the perceived bias of the court against the defense attorney, Dwayne agreed to hire other counsel. In order to bring a new attorney on, the case had to be postponed. During motions to reset the trial for April, a member of the audience made it very clear that they still believed that N. was pregnant, and they predicted her due date might coincide with the new trial.

On 11 February 1994, a motion to dismiss the charges against Dwayne was suddenly filed. Evidently, the doctor who had performed the pregnancy test had not done a vaginal exam—something that should have been required since a man's life and reputation were at stake. The same doctor now confirmed that N. was six or seven months pregnant. Confronted with the test results, N. confessed that she had been involved with someone else and had lied on the witness stand.

Members of the jury who had voted to convict Dwayne had believed N.'s testimony implicitly and were "adamant that N. was an unfortunate little girl who had been robbed of her innocence by a violent and depraved man." As the

Motion to Dismiss stated, this was pivotal to the case against Dwayne.

> During the trial the alleged victim testified that she had not had sexual intercourse with anyone other than the defendant, and that her last sexual contact with the defendant was more than a year prior to the trial. The alleged victim's sexual history was relevant because two doctors testified that their examinations of the alleged victim were consistent with sexual activity.[14]

Dwayne is relieved to be a free man; others have not been as fortunate. His parents, devout Christians, believe that his vindication is an answer to prayer, but their lives will never be the same. The ordeal has been financially devastating for the family, and none of their expenses incurred fighting these false charges will be reimbursed. Dwayne also lost a job because of the ordeal, but the damage to his reputation is more painful. He is naturally concerned that in the minds of some people, there may always be a little doubt regarding his innocence. Nothing can give them back the last year and a half of their lives.

It could have been worse. Because one juror, a man of conviction, was willing to stand up against pressure from his peers, an innocent man is free.

Chapter Eleven

Wards of the State

"Lo, children are an heritage of the Lord: and the fruit of the womb is his reward." (Ps. 127:3)

"Train up a child in the way he should go: and when he is old, he will not depart from it." (Prov. 22:6)

"Children, obey your parents in the Lord: for this is right.

Honour thy father and mother; which is the first commandment with promise; that it may be well with thee, and thou mayest live long on the earth. And, ye fathers, provoke not your children to wrath: but bring them up in the nurture and admonition of the Lord." (Eph. 6:1-4)

The Bible clearly delegates the responsibility of child rearing to the parents: not the community or state, just the parents. Our nation's history is steeped in this Judeo-Christian tradition of family, and the sovereignty of the home was accepted by our Founding Fathers. Though parental rights are not specifically delineated in the Constitution, they are protected by the Fourteenth Amendment. Case law has also reaffirmed the intent of the framers of this document that the family be regarded as beyond the domain of the government. In *Parham v. J.R.,* U.S. 584 (1979), the Supreme Court ruled:

> That some parents "may at times be acting against the best interests of their children" . . . creates a basis for caution, but it is hardly a reason to discard wholesale those pages of human experience that teach that parents generally do act in the child's best interest.

> The statist notion that governmental power should supersede parental authority in *all* cases because

some parents abuse and neglect children is repug-
nant to American tradition.[1]

Redefining the Family

In spite of this American tradition, there is a strong
movement to redefine the family, an issue that received
much attention during the 1992 presidential elections.
The concept of a monogamous, heterosexual family is
laughed at by liberal politicians, media, and the public
school system. Stay-at-home moms are portrayed as dino-
saurs, a fading remnant of male suppression—an opinion
that ignores the growing number of women who are opt-
ing to put their careers on hold and raise a family.

The school system has been deeply involved in "re-
educating" young people to a new concept of family.
Heather Has Two Mommys and *Daddy's Roommate*, two beginning readers, were designed to introduce homosexual
liaisons as acceptable family alternatives. Health textbooks
define family as any group of people living together. As
the children progress through grade school, they are
bombarded with promiscuous propaganda, disguised as
education, intended to further erode parental authority.
Parents supposedly have the right to withdraw their children from sex education, yet in practice this is difficult to
do. For one thing, parents are not always notified, and
many are uninformed of the content of such programs.
Remembering the innocuous, informational films they
were shown in segregated sessions as school kids, they
naively expect the current programs to be similar in content. Parents who do pull their children out of such classes
are in danger of being turned in to CPS for sexual abuse.
Some risk assessment guidelines actually tell teachers and
social workers to be suspicious of any parent who objects
to such curriculum.

These programs are not harmless. One fifth grade
school in Colorado had a mixed sex-ed session where
condoms were handed out to the girls. After detailed
explanations of their use, the boys were instructed to
hold two or three fingers up to simulate a penis. Then the

girls were commanded to open the condom, pick out a boy, and place the condom on his fingers. One parent complained that her daughter came home terribly traumatized by the incident. *This* is child abuse, yet this is condoned by the system.

Many programs blatantly promote the homosexual lifestyle. In Commerce City, Colorado, a guest speaker from the Hall of Life (connected to a city museum) was invited to teach sex education to kids who were too young to legally engage in such activities. Yet, he told the mixed group of students that there are three kinds of sexual activity: homosexual, heterosexual, and sodomy. All forms were acceptable, and they were free to choose to become sexually active whenever they felt like it. The only request he had, of course, was that they use condoms.

Other "health" textbooks promote premarital sex, lesbianism, adultery, and masturbation. One book tells students that "'research shows that homosexuals can lead lives that are as full and healthy as those of heterosexuals.' The statement is under a picture of two men embracing."[2] The book does not warn the kids that homosexual activities would place them at greater risk for the deadly disease AIDS.

Michigan adopted a program that would even meet the approval of Dr. Jocelyn Elders. The Michigan Model, as it is called, promotes explicit sexual instruction for children beginning at age five. Fifth-graders, ten- and eleven-year-old kids, are expected to write essays describing their sexual experiences and are shown films on masturbation.[3] Another Michigan school was sued for teaching seventh through eleventh grade students techniques of masturbation and "descriptions of sexual fantasies involving group and homosexual acts."[4]

A Question of Values

Students are taught to question their parents' values, and to accept the values offered by liberal educators. If parents object when their children adopt promiscuous lifestyles pushed at them by the school system, the child is encouraged to turn the parents in to the child-savers.

The parents of a fourteen-year-old girl in Denver discovered that their young daughter was pregnant. Naturally upset, they grounded her from seeing the boy she had been dating. The daughter simply turned her parents in to Social Services and was immediately placed into foster care. The caseworker told the parents that the daughter would remain in foster care until her baby was born because she was old enough to choose her own friends. The parents' objections revealed unreasonable expectations and inadequate parenting skills, she claimed. Children should be given choices, not rules. The caseworker then set up unsupervised time for the girl to see her boyfriend. During one weekend, shortly before the baby was born, the boyfriend assaulted the pregnant girl—something the parents warned might happen. Though the parents have been told they no longer have any authority over their child, they are still liable for all costs involved, including five thousand dollars for foster care.

Social workers believe kids need to be given choices, not values. Some of these kids spend their entire childhood in foster care, yet the prevailing philosophy is that "we can't impose values on the kids. We can't say, don't have sex. But we can say, have responsible sex." Because of this philosophy, there is a growing push to encourage girls as young as twelve who come into the system to get Norplant. Although this involves surgery, parents are not notified because it is birth control. Group homes promote Norplant as a red badge of courage—a sign of maturity. Girls are told that this is the "responsible" thing to do. If a child does become pregnant, she is taken to Planned Parenthood to discuss her "options." Once again, parental notification is considered unnecessary.

A Christian social worker described this battle of values as one of the biggest problems of the system.

> We can't forget that our kids are children. They are impressionable. We can't expect them to act like adults. Someone has to teach them values or they will end up as street people. Nobody out there in Social Services, especially those who aren't

Christians, wants to hold anyone to any absolute values. That is why abortion is okay. That's why promiscuity is okay. We don't really like it, but it's their choice.

I personally feel like there is no hope for any of our kids without Christ. I try to use my authority to place kids in a Christian or moral homes, and to shut down inappropriate homes. But, I do a lot of bandaid work.

This same caseworker stated that most of the social workers she knew cared about children and that is why they were there. But, their work was affected by their values. In her city, a very large percentage of caseworkers are gay, and this lifestyle has a definite impact on their casework. If someone objects to improper activities in a homosexual foster home, they are labeled as homophobic, and the charges are not thoroughly investigated. These caseworkers will often place allegedly molested children under the care of homosexual therapists who introduce the child to masturbation and homosexual options.

In some cases, this orientation has prevented children from getting counseling they desperately need. One caseworker went before the placement evaluation team to ask for additional money for counseling for a foster child assigned to him. He felt the counseling was important because the girl was being very difficult and engaging in some masculine types of behaviors, such as trying to shave her face. He told the committee that the foster parents were trying to help her with these identity issues and to build up her self-esteem as a woman, but they felt the need for professional assistance. However, the lesbian director denied the funds. "This child is entering adolescence, and she may be homosexual," she said. "You cannot have the foster parent promote heterosexuality if this child wants to choose a different way."

Anti-Christian Bias

There is strong anti-Christian sentiment among many CPS workers. Christians are known to believe in corporal punishment, which is tantamount to abuse in child-saver circles. Christians are also seen as rigid and intolerant, unfit to rear children for the New World Order. Homosexual workers, aware of the Christian teachings regarding their lifestyle, are often very hostile to parents who openly display their faith. The New York State Council of Family and Child Caring Agencies (CFCCA) warns that parents who resist state interference, believe in spanking, or display an "'over involvement in religion'" are suspect.[5]

Home school parents often encounter this same bias. Many parents teach their children at home for religious reasons. They consider it a God-given responsibility to provide their children's education, and they object to the humanistic philosophy taught by the state. To the average child-saver who views children as community property, this is particularly offensive. One low-income Christian mother was ordered to have a psychiatric evaluation after her daughter was abducted from school by CPS because of an alleged spanking. (The girl was interrogated for eight hours, and transcripts show that she repeatedly denied any abusive treatment, yet she was placed in foster care. The terrified mother was not notified until ten o'clock that night.)

The psychiatrist who examined this mother questioned her extensively on her religious beliefs, asking questions such as "Do you believe Jesus is the Son of God?" "Do you believe people can heal by laying on hands?" "Do you believe that Christ will return?" At this point, the mother said, "I believed we had religious freedom. Why are you asking these questions?"

The psychiatrist replied, "Because certain religious beliefs prejudice you against being a good parent. For example, do you believe in 'Spare the rod, spoil the child'?" Knowing that social workers generally view this passage as a biblical mandate for child abuse, the mother tried to answer as carefully as possible. She explained that the verse in question was a proverb, or principle, and that it simply meant that children who grew up without discipline became spoiled. She went on to explain that God was a God of love, that all discipline should be administered in love, and nowhere in the Bible did God condone hurting a child. At that point, the court-ordered psychiatrist looked at the Christian mother and replied, "If you believe that, you are an unfit parent."

The Anti-Family Agenda

Dr. James Hitchcock, professor of history at St. Louis University describes what he calls an "Antifamily Revolution."

> It would be only a slight exaggeration to say that American society is increasingly coming to be divided between those who accept the family and those who reject it and indeed even hate it. The former are still in the majority. However, as with so many other moral revolutions of recent times, the minority which hates the family has managed to get itself strategically ensconced—in the mass media, in the educational system, in many private social agencies, and most importantly in government. . . . Although various parts of it have been experienced, the remarkable fact has not been noticed that in the past fifteen years the sacred bonds constituting all the most basic human relationships have been systematically broken, to the point where no human links of any kind are any longer regarded as inviolable.[6]

Strong families are one of the biggest stumbling blocks to educating children for a global community. For most kids, the home is the place where their values are formed. Because of this, those who wish to usher in a New World Order must be able to monitor and dictate the values of the next generation. To achieve this goal, it is important that parental authority be remanded to the state.

There is a growing belief that parenting is not a private act, it is a social act which should be monitored. One CPS supervisor told a class of aspiring home health aides that "Children do not belong to their parents. They belong to the Universe."

This sentiment is echoed by prominent members of the child abuse industry. James Garbarino, an "expert" who believes all corporal punishment is abuse, has this advice for fellow child-savers:

> We do indeed have a big agenda in changing this orientation, an orientation that says that children are the private matter of their parents. We have to see that child rearing is a social matter and that being a parent is a social act.[7]

Elizabeth Robinson, a clinical psychologist, explains that child rearing "is not a private matter between only the parent and child. It is important to all of us how that child is raised. This is tomorrow. This is our future."[8] Sociologist Alice Rossi takes the argument even further, claiming that the human species has reached a point in its evolution where parenting must become a community act and that it is "unnatural" for people to parent on their own or in nuclear families.[9]

Parents' Rights vs. Children's Rights

There is a prevailing misconception that the rights of parents and children are somehow incompatible. Parents are selfish, incapable of placing their children's needs ahead of their own. The right of parents to promote values, set guidelines, enforce discipline, limit social contacts, and make educational choices is under attack. Common law recognized that minor children do not have the knowledge, experience, or maturity to make many decisions, which is why God gave them parents. Child protection laws that limit a child's employment, sexual activities, and purchasing habits have been created to protect young people from unscrupulous people who would abuse them; child rights advocates wish to repeal these restrictions.

In a 1979 article published in *Children's Rights: Contemporary Perspectives*, Hillary Clinton (then Rodham) wrote, "Children should have a right to be permitted to decide their own future if they are competent." Because current law does not recognize underage children as competent, Mrs. Clinton proposed that we should "reverse the presumption of incompetency and instead assume all individuals are competent until proven otherwise."

The First Lady, who supports children's rights, insists that these comments were made in the context of child abuse. But, such changes would have far-reaching consequences. In spite of her denials, "deciding their own future" would extend to choices of friends, schooling, abortion, living arrangements, contracts, and a myriad of other decisions. It would be the state, through courts and child protective services, who would determine when a a child is "competent"; not the parent who knows the child better than anyone else. This is simply one more move to destroy the family.

CPS Goes to School

Child protection workers are becoming very involved in the school, viewing it as a center for social change. Public schools are a prime source for CPS referrals and a convenient place to apprehend children without the interference of the parent. Some schools utilize "journaling" as a method of determining what activities occur in the home. Grade school children are asked to write journals, answering such questions as "What do your parents fight about?" "What do you talk about at home?" "What activities do you do as a family?" "What don't you like about your parents?" "If you were a parent, and your child disobeyed, how would you discipline him?" Some of these questions are private and inappropriate as a school assignment. Answers regarding discipline are taken as testimony regarding disciplinary measures that are occurring in the home. Yet, the answers are quite often simply the creation of a creative, and possibly mischievous, child.

For one family, journaling came with a twelve-thousand-dollar price tag. Their emotionally ill daughter was under the care of a child psychologist. Her grade school teacher required the students to write daily in their journals. One day, the student wrote that her stepfather was molesting her. Needless to say, she did not go home that night. When the family appeared in court, the attending psychologist testified that the child was emotionally disturbed and a chronic liar. He added that she frequently made outlandish accusations to get attention and that, in his opinion, nothing had occurred; but, CPS would not consider this option. After all, children *never* lie. Without any medical evidence to verify possible sexual abuse, the girl was placed into foster care and the family was ordered into "therapy."

Spurred on by the attention, the girl wove fantastic stories of abuse in her journal. Every tale was believed until, bored with just one villain, the child began to accuse the teacher, principal, school board members, and the social worker of also molesting her. Suddenly, CPS and the school decided that in this one case, a child could lie, and returned the girl to her family. By this time, the parents had spent twelve thousand dollars on legal and counseling fees, none of which was reimbursed.

In Colorado, a constitutional amendment was defeated which would have set up social service offices in every school in the state. Undaunted by its defeat, Denver is experimenting with two model programs that will result in every six-year-old enrolled in the Denver public schools to be interviewed by a social worker.

Wards of the State

Inflated statistics about child abuse are used to convince the public of the overall incompetence of American adults to parent without the overseeing eye of Uncle Sam. Based on this erroneous premise, the state sees government involvement in the life of every child prior to birth as a way to prevent abuse issues, solve educational deficiencies, and create properly socialized world citizens. Under the guise of Education 2000, many states are recommending prenatal and early childhood home visits to make certain that the parent's philosophy and discipline meet the social worker's standards and to guarantee that the child will receive "proper" stimulation, thereby preparing him for a successful school career. What these programs really do is allow CPS agents to visit every home and arbitrarily determine, according to their own personal standards and prejudices, who is and is not fit to be a parent.

According to the NCPCA, successful child abuse prevention programs include universal provision of services to *all* new parents, services that begin at or before birth, and screening *all births* for "high risk characteristics."[10]

New York has developed an invasive home visit program that meets these criteria. Their Prenatal and Postnatal Parent Education hospital program was instituted by the New York State Citizens Task Force on Child Abuse. This program, under the joint leadership of Matilda Cuomo and state commissioner of Social Services, Cesar Perales, operates on a three-part plan: 1) Prenatal, when the prospective mother is given literature regarding health care. 2) Delivery phase, first prenatal exam after going to hospital. There a team of professionals, including a pediatrician, primary care nurse, obstetrician or nurse-midwife, social worker or psychologist, and a nutritionist "closely but discreetly scrutinize her for any problems she *might* have" [Emphasis added] (as though women are always at their best in labor), and 3) Postnatal, which includes regular follow-up home visits.[11]

Though the new mother is unaware of the process, she is being scrutinized while in the hospital to determine if she is a competent parent or if she falls into a "high risk" category. She is judged on her confidence about becoming a mother, if she acts depressed after delivery (which could be caused by the hormonal change), and whether or not the father comes to visit.

Postnatal visits are great opportunities for social workers to enter the home on fishing expeditions. Home visitors go into the young mother's home on a regular basis and "ask how she is doing, casting an alert eye around the household to judge the situation for herself."[12]

Dr. Fontana, a child abuse "expert" from New York who believes abuse occurs in almost every home, would like the program to be adopted nationwide and given even greater authority. His suggestions include requiring hospitals to do an assessment on *every woman* who gives birth in a hospital to determine if she should even be allowed to take the child home. Postnatal visits should be used to enforce his ideas of discipline and to abolish all forms of corporal punishment.

Children's Bill of Rights

The Supreme Court has generally ruled in favor of the constitutional protection of the family, which is one of the driving forces behind the move to adopt the United Nations Covenant on the Rights of the Child. As an international treaty, this covenant would supersede the Constitution as the law of the land and effectively eliminate the Fourteenth Amendment protection of the family.

The United Nations Covenant on the Rights of the Child was approved on 19 November 1989 by the UN General Assembly. It has since been ratified by at least seventy countries, but not by the United States. However, pressure is mounting to get the document before Congress. The Children's Defense Fund, a leading child rights activist group, has indicated support for the treaty. Until recently, Hillary Clinton served on the CDF board, and it appears likely that President Bill Clinton would sign such a treaty if it could get congressional approval. A resolution (SR70) has been introduced into the U.S. Senate to ratify the UN Convention.

Children's books and youth sections of the newspaper tout the Rights of the Child as a loving, reasonable guarantee for humane treatment for all young people. But, the covenant goes much, much further, destroying any vestige of parental authority and leaving children vulnerable to destructive influences. Hitler saw the importance of capturing the minds and values of the younger generation, and his tactics proved highly successful. Those who are promoting a global community are following in his footsteps.

The covenant argued that parents often do not put their children's needs first, so it is incumbent upon the state to become the guardian and protector of all children. The resolution they passed contains fifty-four articles designed to usurp the role of parents. In Article One, responsibility for the child is vested in the state. Article Two prevents parents from disciplining their children for actions that are contrary to the parent's values. Children are to have the freedom to set their own values without their parents' imposition. The resolution also recognizes the state as co-parent and requires children to attend state-run schools, institutions, facilities, and services. It is the state that will determine medical (and psychological) treatment for all children, and the parents may not interfere. Article Thirteen proclaims that children have the right to "seek, receive, and impart information and ideas of all kinds . . . either orally, in writing or in print, in the form of art, or through any other media of the child's choice." This includes pornography.

Article Twenty-eight of the resolution denies the parent's right to home school and forbids any form of corporal punishment. Article Fifteen grants children the right to "freedom of association." In other words, parents have no say in their child's choice of companions, including gang membership. Entering a child's room without permission would be considered a violation of his right to privacy and restricting access to TV would be forbidden. God entrusted parents with the spiritual training of their children, the United Nations resolution would transfer this responsibility to the mass media!

Throughout the document, parents are continually viewed as mere baby sitters under the control of the state. The resolution demands that its articles be given full force of the law, and parents who refuse to comply may be prosecuted. Proponents of children's rights hail this document as a stepping stone to adopting an even more liberal legislation. Not surprisingly, the National Education Association also supports this movement, and, in an advertisement paid for by NEA dues in 1992, association president Keith Geiger promoted his own proposed Bill of Rights for Children.[13]

The extent of the child rights agenda is apparent in Richard Farson's Children's Bill of Rights. He proposes the following:

1. The Right of Self-Determination. Children should
   have the right to decide matters which affect them
   directly. [Sounds like Hillary Clinton.]
2. The Right to Alternate Home Environments.
3. The Right to Responsive Design [child-size facili-
   ties].
4. The Right to Information.
5. The Right to Educate Oneself.
6. The Right to Freedom from Physical Punishment.
7. The Right to Sexual Freedom.
8. The Right to Economic Power.
9. The Right to Justice.[14]

In his explanation of these "rights," Farson insists
that children be allowed to decide if they wish to go to
school or not, where they want to live, have access to all
pornography, be able to make binding contracts, to sue
their parents, and to have sex with adults at any age.[15] In
reality, this is a call to decriminalize child rape and exploi-
tation.

In Ephesians 6:12, we are warned that "we wrestle not
against flesh and blood, but against principalities, against
powers, against the rulers of darkness of this world, against
spiritual wickedness in high places." Spiritual warfare has
been declared against the family. It's time concerned
parents become involved in stopping these dangerous
encroachments.

Chapter Twelve

A Call for Change

Child Protective Services is out of control. The system, as it operates today, should be scrapped. If children are to be protected in their homes and in the system, radical new guidelines must be adopted.

At the core of the problem is the antifamily mindset of CPS. Removal is the first resort, not the last. With insufficient checks and balances, the system that was designed to protect children has become the greatest perpetrator of harm. What is required is a change of philosophy; a recognition that parents are better equipped to care for children than the state. This chapter identifies several areas of change that, if incorporated, could help to protect the abused child and still preserve families.

Federal Changes

Currently, federal funding favors removal of children from their homes over family preservation. In an attempt to change that philosophy, the Adoption Assistance Child Welfare Act (Public Law 996-272) required that "reasonable efforts" be made to preserve families, yet that clause has never been actively enforced. In order for family preservation to succeed, these changes must be made at the federal level.

1. "Reasonable efforts" must be defined and guidelines established to ensure the enforcement of this clause. Currently, judges often only require the caseworker's affirmation that such efforts have been made, a practice that has resulted in much abuse. Caseworkers must be required to file a report, in writing, detailing the efforts

they made to keep the family together. In addition, families must be allowed the right to contest the validity of the reports.

2. Family preservation goals receive lip service in DPS departmental guidelines, but, in practice, most departments are extremely hostile to the idea. Out-of-home placement is generally the first option, not the last. In order to make counties practice what they preach, funding should be withheld from any state that does not have a family preservation program.

3. Funding provisions for special child abuse prosecutors should be altered. The use of these special prosecutors tends to create "cause attorneys" who lack the objectivity more easily sustained by prosecutors who handle a variety of cases. Such funding creates a great imbalance for the accused, who must fight against vast resources with his own limited funds. These funds should be split to help provide for impartial investigation of alleged abuse, a move that might even reduce costs by keeping more unfounded cases out of court.

4. The blanket immunity now afforded those who report abuse should be amended to provide for prosecuting those who blatantly use the system for their own revenge. Anonymous reporting should no longer be encouraged, and such reports should never be considered grounds for entering a home or removing a child. It is insulting for the government to believe that American citizens care so little for their young that they would only report serious abuse anonymously.

Members of the child abuse industry hide behind a curtain of confidentiality designed more to protect themselves than to protect the child. This should be altered to only apply to the public disclosure of the names of juveniles. Currently, confidentiality is being used to conceal evidence and to protect CPS from lawsuits. Citizens should be allowed to sue for redress when CPS workers, therapists, and juvenile courts violate due process, commit perjury, and engage in professional misconduct.

5. The government should refrain from meddling in the schools, criminalizing spanking, and regulating home schools. Efforts to establish a national school board or set standards for teachers and home schools violate the limitations placed on the federal government by the Constitution. At this time, interference is rampant. Examples include bills such as H.R. 1522, introduced in 1992 to prohibit corporal punishment for any organization that receives federal funding. This would set a precedent for categorizing spanking as a form of child abuse.

In early 1994, H.R. 6, a reauthorization of the Elementary and Secondary Education Act, was placed before the U.S. House of Representatives. This seven hundred-plus page bill sought to expand control of the federal government over public, private, and home schools by requiring that *all* teachers meet state certification requirements. The thrust of the bill was to mandate, at a federal level, the essential elements of outcome-based education. An additional, late amendment was added by Rep. George Miller (D-CA) which provides:

> ASSURANCE.—Each State applying for funds under this title shall provide the Secretary with the assurance that after July 1, 1998, it will require each local educational agency within the State to certify that each full time teacher in schools under the jurisdiction of the agency is certified to teach in the subject area to which he or she is assigned.

This would have essentially eliminated most home schools and many private schools. Teachers at private schools have often graduated from nonaccredited private colleges, which, in many states, prevents them from being certified. While it could be argued that this bill was not intended to interfere with private education, all doubts were erased when Rep. Dick Armey (R-TX) proposed an amendment that stated, "Nothing in this title shall be construed to authorize or encourage Federal control over the curriculum or practices of any private, religious, or home school." The amendment was defeated on straight party lines. These efforts, among others, represent the government's efforts to usurp a parent's control over his child's education. However, public outcry is still an effective weapon against such encroachments. Outraged citizens demanded that an amendment be added to except home and private schools, and they won.

Preserving Due Process

The following changes would help preserve the constitutional right of due process for the accused.

1. State statutes need to be revised to more precisely define abuse and neglect.

2. Anonymous tips should not be considered grounds for intervention. Confidentiality laws are currently being misconstrued as a means of perverting justice and protecting the system. Anyone accused of child abuse should have the right to face the accuser. Hearsay evidence has been banned in other civil and criminal courts, it should be banned in juvenile court as well.

3. Every interrogation of a child should be videotaped in its entirety, and a copy of that tape should be made immediately available to the defendant. CPS workers should not be allowed to badger the child, relentlessly pursuing an accusation. The child should be allowed to have a friendly adult advocate of the child's choice whenever he or she is questioned or required to submit to any type of examination. If a videotaped testimony is going to be used in court, then a representative of the accused should be allowed to participate in the questioning of the witness.

4. The use of polygraphs, penile plethysmographs, anatomical dolls, and aggressive questioning should be banned. Companies who market the plethysmograph and its accompanying photographs should be shut down for profiting in child pornography.

5. Confidentiality laws are being abused to protect CPS from proper investigation. These laws should only limit revealing the names of the parties involved.

6. There must be accountability within the system. Independent review boards should be set up in each state to hear complaints from parents and other parties who have been accused. These boards must not be hampered by the curtain of confidentiality and should be empowered to call witnesses, subpoena all records, and review the actions of CPS. Social workers who lie in court or deliberately distort the facts should be charged with perjury and dismissed from their jobs. Prosecutors, social workers, and therapists who deliberately conceal evidence that might exonerate the accused should be charged with obstruction of justice.

7. Child protective agencies should be stripped of their police powers. If an initial screening of a complaint indicates that further investigation is warranted, then the case should be turned over to police officers trained in objective investigation. At all times, the rights of the accused, as well as the alleged victim, should be respected.

8. Children should only be removed from their homes if their physical safety is seriously jeopardized by remaining home during the investigative stage. Family preservation should be attempted in all but the most violent cases. Currently, if a child is removed from home, the law generally requires a hearing within forty-eight hours to determine if placement is appropriate. However, these hearings only last an average of three to ten minutes and are a mockery of justice. In practice, the judge will rubber stamp the recommendations of the caseworker, and the parent may not even be allowed to speak in their own behalf or bring forth witnesses to refute the accusations. As a result, very few children are returned at this time, and it may be months before the next hearing.

This practice must be changed. If parents were allowed to present a defense at the first hearing, months of traumatic separation and incredible expense could be avoided. And, if family preservation were practiced first, the courts would have more time.

9. In the case of a charge of sexual abuse, if the accused parent leaves the house, the child should be allowed to remain in the home, in the custody of the other parent.

10. If a child is removed from the home, relatives should receive first consideration for foster care.

11. While in foster care, daily phone calls and visits should be allowed. (Visits are often used as a weapon, something to be earned by good behavior. This attitude denies the importance of family preservation and is incredibly abusive to a child who is missing his family.)

12. Children in foster care should be placed as close to home as possible, and siblings should be placed together whenever possible. If this option is not available, then visits between siblings should be arranged. Foster parents should be instructed that any interference with visitation would be considered grounds to remove the child from the home.

13. Eliminate the policy of some counties to require therapy for everyone entering the system. If therapy is required, then the choice of the specialist should be left to the parent.

14. Eliminate standard strip-search as part of the initial interview. Children are horribly traumatized by being stripped, photographed, and poked at by a stranger.

15. Instruct that CPS will operate under an assumption of *innocence* until guilt is proven.

16. The charge of educational neglect should be dropped.

17. CPS should not be allowed to order separations or divorce without a hearing.

18. No name should be placed on the Central Registry until he or she has willingly confessed to abuse or until he or she has been found guilty. Names should not be placed on the registry without a hearing. If another court finds the accused not guilty or if no charges are going to be filed, then the name doesn't belong on the list. Also, children should not be placed on the registry as

possible future offenders simply because they have been victimized.

19. Allow the accused the right to choose his own counsel, his experts, and review all the evidence.

20. Require higher educational requirements of therapists and social workers and stricter standards for foster homes.

Whenever the topic of change comes up, child-savers always insist that money is the cure. However, if children were not inappropriately placed, there would be sufficient funding. As the San Diego grand jury concluded, the system does not need to expand. It has plenty of money; it just needs to redirect how that money is spent.

The current CPS system is morally bankrupt, and drastic changes are required to protect children and families.

Chapter Thirteen

The Best Defense

"Behold, I send you forth as sheep in the midst of wolves: be ye therefore wise as serpents and harmless as doves" (Matt. 10:16).

No one is immune from the intrusiveness of child protective agencies, yet there are some steps that can be taken to avoid unwarranted intervention. The first step is to live a lifestyle that is above reproach. The Bible warns, "Abstain from all appearance of evil"—wise advice for those wishing to remain *outside* the system. Live-in lovers, excessive use of alcohol, or a turbulent family life may all be warning flags to social workers.

Another way to protect your family is to avoid dependence upon governmental agencies. It is important to help the needy and to make certain children have food to eat, but, in our society, welfare has become more than a hand up; it has become a way of life. A recent Rainbow Coalition conference aggressively promoted books that instructed them on how to tap into every available government program, from getting food stamps to having Uncle Sam pay for your house.

Once a person accepts funds from a social agency, however, he has opened himself up for unprecedented meddling. Recipients may be required to have home visits. Children on WIC (Women, Infants, and Children) are examined and weighed to determine if they are "failure to thrive." This term is supposed to apply to children in the bottom of the weight chart who are lethargic, unhealthy, and not growing at their expected rate. This

condition can be the result of immune system deficiencies, premature birth, digestive disorders, numerous
medical problems, as well as fetal alcohol syndrome or
lack of care. However, in many cases social workers interpret "failure to thrive" as meaning any child who is in the
bottom 5 percent of the weight chart for their age, even
if the child is healthy, energetic, and comes from parents
who are also small. They assume that any child who is in
the bottom 10 percent of a weight chart based on Anglo-
Saxon children is neglected. One family lost their healthy
daughter when she was classified "failure to thrive" by a
caseworker, even though they brought in documentation
to prove that the child was part Korean—a fact that accounted for her small stature.

Avoiding the School Trap

There is a movement to bring social services into
every school based upon a "one-stop shopping" concept.
What is really behind the program is an ambitious campaign to usurp the role of the parent. Schools are the
source of a large percentage of social service referrals.
Children in public school are frequently told that they
have a right to disagree with their parents, that parents
should not be allowed to force their own values upon the
children, and that discipline is taboo. If a parent engages
in any form of discipline the child dislikes, he simply has
to turn the parent in to the school social worker. A Denver mother who became frustrated with her fourteen-
year-old daughter's disobedience and rebellion finally
grounded the girl from using the telephone for one month.
The next day the teenager complained at school and she
was escorted by a social worker to a foster home. The
caseworker insisted that such "abusive" punishment for
blatant disobedience was unwarranted and that the parents needed to be reeducated. In order to get their daughter back, they had to agree to a "treatment plan" that
included, of course, psychiatric counseling and parenting
classes where they were taught that fourteen-year-old chil-

dren are old enough to make their own choices without parental involvement. The child remained in foster care for six months, and the parents and taxpayers received the bill.

Another invasive devise spreading across the nation that is supported by public schools and legislators such as Rep. Patricia Schroeder (D-CO) is the Parents as First Teachers (PAT) program. Originally developed in Missouri, PAT has been introduced in at least forty states. The purpose of the program was to screen potentially disadvantaged children and offer assistance to assure that they will have the same opportunity to succeed as their wealthier classmates. This sounds like a noble objective, but, in reality, it is simply one more move to destroy parental authority.

In this program, a home visitor—sometimes called a "parent educator"—is assigned to a family. They visit the home frequently, tell the parents which forms of discipline they are allowed to use (spanking, of course, is forbidden), help the family apply for any government programs that they may need, and of course, insist that the children attend *public* schools where they can be monitored. In some states, all participating children are listed in computers as "at risk," regardless of their home situation, giving CPS workers ready access to the child at all times. If a child exhibits behavior problems, CPS will recommend medical and/or psychiatric treatment. Parents are discouraged from getting outside opinions, and failure to comply with CPS treatment plans can result in removal of the child.

Families are recruited for these programs from health clinics, hospitals, and welfare and social service agencies. Any child who can be deemed "at risk" is a candidate, and the guidelines for this category are written so broadly that *every child* qualifies. (Some PAT proponents advocate extending the program to every home.) In Missouri, risk factors taken from official CPS lists, include:

1. Illness or handicapping condition at birth.
2. Signs of failure to thrive.
3. Delay in *any area* of development detected through observation and screening.
4. Inability of parent to cope with inappropriate child behavior.
5. Low functioning parent (due to limited ability or illness).
6. Inability of parent to relate to or connect with child.
7. Overindulgence, undue spoiling on part of parent.
8. Low level of verbal response or communication with child.
9. Negative or hostile behavior toward child.
10. Undue stress that adversely affects family functioning.
11. Indication of child abuse.
12. *Other* [emphasis added].[1]

This is a blatant attack on the family, and parents would do well to opt out of all involvement with PAT or its clones. Parents should become involved in exposing programs such as this. School board elections, generally ignored by the majority of voters, are vitally important. Even people who do not have children in public schools have a vested interest in this encroachment on liberty.

Many parents have decided the best way to prevent their families from becoming a statistic is to avoid public schools altogether, turning to private or home schools instead. For those who choose to educate their children at home, membership in the Home School Legal Defense Association is a valuable safeguard. For a reasonable annual fee, parents have emergency access to an attorney in the event that a social worker or truant officer appears at their door. In addition, HSLDA attorneys serve as watchdogs challenging antagonistic legislation both at the state and national levels. More information about this helpful organization may be obtained by writing:

Home School Legal Defense Association
P.O. Box 159
Paeonian Springs, VA 22129

A Matter of Discipline

Children can act up in public, and obedience should be required in all settings, but a parent who spanks a child in public may be courting disaster. Numerous families have been surprised to find a social worker at their door because someone saw them swat their child, took down their license number, and reported them for abuse. When used according to the guidelines discussed earlier, spanking can be an appropriate form of discipline, but it should be used in the privacy of the home.

HSLDA attorney Christopher Klicka recommends that parents who are questioned about discipline avoid using verses that are often misconstrued by child-savers, such as "Spare the rod, spoil the child." A Denver social worker confirmed that such comments generally brand the parent as an abusive religious fanatic. Instead, Klicka suggests that parents describe their philosophy of discipline in very general terms and to use positive verses, such as Matthew 18:6, that are not as easily twisted or misunderstood by caseworkers.[2]

When CPS Comes Calling

If a social worker shows up at the door, it is important to view the situation seriously, no matter how ridiculous or unbelievable the inquiries may seem. It is quite natural for innocent parents with nothing to hide to open their doors freely to this intrusion, convinced that any reasonable person will see that the complaint is unfounded. But, the typical CPS worker is not reasonable; they assume that the accused is guilty. In the event of such a visit, the following guidelines, which are not meant to be legal advice, may help keep a family from being sucked into the destructive CPS system.

1. No matter how offensive the situation is, be polite. The caseworker does not know you, and a natural, angry

reaction is generally viewed as proof of an abusive personality.

2. Do *not* allow the social worker or police officer to enter the home unless they have a warrant issued by a court. Politely but firmly insist that they stay outside. No matter what the caseworker may tell you, the Fourth Amendment protection against illegal search and seizure *does* apply to social workers and police officers alike, and warrants are only supposed to be issued if there is probable cause—anonymous tips don't qualify.

If parents do choose to let the social worker in the home, caselaw confirms that they have voluntarily waived their Fourth Amendment rights. And, a CPS agent on a mission may find a dirty sock on the floor, dishes in the sink, or some other "unacceptable" condition resulting in the removal of the children.

3. *Never* allow the social worker to interview children alone. Children may be traumatized by the experience, and even the most innocent answers may be twisted or blatantly misrepresented by a caseworker on a fishing expedition.

4. The social worker may have genuine concern over the welfare of the child, so it is important to reassure them that everything is fine. Allow the children to come to the window or screen door where the social worker can see them and be reassured. Klicka recommends that parents be willing to take their children to the family doctor to be examined and have the doctor submit a letter confirming that they are okay. Additionally, letters of reference from neighbors or other professionals that know the family can be sent to the caseworker as well.

5. If an interview is required, the parents, not the children, should arrange for the meeting to be held at the CPS agency, not the home. If possible, it may be helpful to have an attorney present.

6. Insist upon your constitutional rights. There is no reason a person should be required to submit to polygraphs or penile plethysmography.

7. In many cases, this may be sufficient to resolve any problem. If the probing continues, it is vital to get an attorney who is familiar with the child abuse industry. The V.O.C.A.L. office in the area should be able to recommend lawyers with expertise in this area.

8. Contact a V.O.C.A.L. office (Victims of Child Abuse Laws). Contrary to CPS propaganda, this organization does not exist to shield child abusers. They do care about children and feel that they should be protected form abuse, both from their parents and from the system. V.O.C.A.L. can be a valuable resource.

9. Tape record all conversations with CPS. (Check your state laws to see if the other party is required to be notified.) There is a very inexpensive device available for recording phone calls as well. This helps to prevent conversations from being twisted or taken out of context. It also gives the accused proof of any threats made by the caseworker.

10. An innocent party should never accept a plea bargain, no matter how tempting it may seem. In CPS circles, a "no contest" plea equates to guilt. Also, the judges are not bound to any offers made by the caseworker or prosecuting attorney, and they will often insist on an evaluation by a court-appointed therapist. When the accused explains that he is innocent, the therapist may tell the court that the accused is unrepentant and in denial. Many have found a plea bargain a quick path to jail or loss of their children.

11. If charges are being pursued, it is important to hire an investigator to investigate the accused, the alleged victim, and the accuser.

12. If a child is examined for investigation of abuse, immediately take him or her to be reexamined by the physician known to the family.

13. If a child is forced to undergo a mental health evaluation, demand that the entire session be videotaped and that the tape be given to the accused. If possible, have an attorney or other advocate present during the evaluation.

14. Do not willingly surrender the children, move out of the home, or do anything that puts the family under CPS control.

Anyone falsely accused of child abuse should vigorously fight to defend their rights. At the same time, no one should live in a state of fear. Christians, in particular, should remember that God is not the author of fear, and "Greater is he that is in you than he that is in the world" (I John 4:4b).

Notes

Chapter One

1. David Grogan and Lorenzo Benet, "A Time for Healing," *People Weekly*, vol. 38, no. 14 (5 October 1992): 134.

2. K. L. Billingsley, "Sex, Lies and County Government: Abuse Case Shows It All," *The San Diego Union Tribune* (19 July 1992): 4C.

3. Ibid.

4. Ibid.

5. *James W. et al. v. The Superior Court of San Diego County*, Certified Court Documents, Court of Appeals, Fourth Appellate District Division One, State of CA, D017377 (Super. Ct. No. 648007), (16 July 1993): 2.

6. Ibid.

7. K. L. Billingsley, "The Scientific War on Child Abuse," *National Review* (15 February 1993): 25.

8. *James W. et al.*, 5.

9. Billingsley, "Sex, Lies and County Government," 4C.

10. *James W. et al.*, 6.

11. Ibid.

12. Ibid.

13. Grogan and Benet, "A Time for Healing," 135.

14. *James W. et al.*, 3.

15. Ibid., 4.

16. Ibid., 3.

17. Billingsley, "Sex, Lies and County Government," 4C.

18. Grogan and Benet, "A Time for Healing," 135.

19. Billingsley, "Sex, Lies and County Government," 4C.

20. Ibid.

Chapter Two

1. *Corrupted Innocence* (CA: V.O.C.A.L., 1992), Video.

2. Murray Levine and Adeline Levine, *Helping Children: A Social History* (New York: Oxford Press, 1992), 207.

3. Ibid.

4. Ibid.

5. Ruth Hubble, *Foster Care and Families* (Philadelphia: Temple University Press, 1981), 46.

6. Levine, *Helping Children: A Social History*, 208.

7. Ronald B. Taylor, *The Kid Business: How It Exploits the Children It Should Help* (Boston: Houghton Mifflin Co., 1981), 80.

8. Ibid.

9. Levine, *Helping Children: A Social History*, 209.

10. Ibid.

11. Ibid., 213.

12. Ibid., 211.

13. Ibid., 212.

14. Ibid., 318-9.

15. *Corrupted Innocence*.

16. Ibid.

Chapter Three

1. *Child Abuse and Neglect Data: AHA Fact Sheet #1* (Englewood, CO: American Humane Society, 1993), 1.

2. Karen McCurdy, *Current Trends in Child Abuse Reporting and Fatalities: The Results of the 1992 Annual Fifty State Survey* (Chicago: National Center on Child Abuse Prevention Research, 1993), 2.

3. *Child Abuse and Neglect Data: AHA Fact Sheet #1*, 1.

4. McCurdy, *Current Trends in Child Abuse Reporting and Fatalities*, 6.

5. Else Green, "Dear Members and Friends," *V.O.C.A.L. News* (November 1993): 1.

6. McCurdy, *Current Trends in Child Abuse Reporting and Fatalities*, 7.

7. Seth Faber, "The Real Abuse," *National Review* (12 April 1993): 47.

8. McCurdy, *Current Trends in Child Abuse Reporting and Fatalities*, 5.

9. Ibid., 7.

10. Ibid., 9.

11. Douglas Besharov, "The Child Abuse Numbers Game," *Wall Street Journal* (4 August 1988).

12. McCurdy, *Current Trends in Child Abuse Reporting and Fatalities*, 12.

13. Ibid., 13.

14. Karen Bailey, "Agencies Have Answers, Lack Funds to Solve Child Abuse Problems," *Rocky Mountain News* (30 October 1986): 45.

15. Julie Szekely, "Report: CPS Violating Rights," *Tucson Citizen* (21 July 1993): 2A.

16. Richard Wexler, *Wounded Innocents* (Buffalo, NY: Prometheus Books, 1990), 17.

17. Besharov, "The Child Abuse Numbers Game."

18. Rebecca Cantwell, "Refresher Course Eyed in Reporting Child Abuse," *Rocky Mountain News* (16 January 1990).

19. Besharov, "The Child Abuse Numbers Game."

20. Wexler, *Wounded Innocents*, 16.

21. Faber, "The Real Abuse," 45.

22. Clancy, Firpo, and Weisinger, *A System Out of Balance*, (CA: 1992), Video.

23. K. L. Billingsley, "Sex. Lies and County Government: Abuse Case Shows It All," *San Diego Union Tribune* (19 June 1992): 4C.

24. *Dollars and Cents of Family Preservation* (New York: Edna McConnell Clark Foundation, 1991).

Chapter Four

1. *Colorado Revised Statutes.*

2. Ibid.

3. Richard Wexler, *Wounded Innocents* (Buffalo, NY: Prometheus Books, 1990), 17.

4. Ibid.

5. L.A., interview with author (December 1993.

6. Wexler, *Wounded Innocents*, 17.

7. *Corrupted Innocence*, (CA: V.O.C.A.L., 1992), Video.

8. Seth Farber, "The Real Abuse," *National Review* (12 April 1993): 47.

9. Ibid.

10. L.A., interview with author.

11. Jane Hulse, "Mom Loses Custody Amid Abuse Charges," *Rocky Mountain News* (26 October 1986): 7.

12. Julie Szekely, "Mom vs. CPS," *Tucson Citizen* (21 October 1993): 1D.

13. Wexler, *Wounded Innocents*, 17.

14. Author's interview with foster parents (name withheld by request) (April 1993).

15. "Who Are the Real Abusers?" *Arizona V.O.C.A.L. Newsletter* (September 1988): 1.

16. Hannah B. Lapp, "America's Child Protective System, Is Justice the Exception Rather Than the Rule?" reprinted in *AFA Journal* (February 1992): 11.

17. Dr. James Dobson, *Hide or Seek* (New Jersey: Fleming H. Revell Co, 1979), 91.

18. Ibid.

19. *Scared Silent*, (USA: National Committee for Prevention of Child Abuse), 10.

20. *Act Now to Prevent Child Abuse* (USA: National Committee for Prevention of Child Abuse).

21. James Garbarino, "Creating a Less Violent Society Can Protect Children from Physical Abuse," in *America's Children: Opposing Viewpoints*, ed. Carol Wekesser (San Diego: Greenhaven Press, 1991), 112.

22. Ibid., 114.

23. Vincent J. Fontana and Valeria Moolman, *Save the Family, Save the Child* (New York: Penquin Books USA, 1991), 103.

24. Ibid., 104–5.

25. Ibid., 104.

26. Ibid., 105.

27. Wexler, *Wounded Innocents*, 443–8.

28. Ibid.

29. Ibid.

30. Ibid., 236–7.

31. Fontana and Moolman, *Save the Family, Save the Child*, 105.

32. L.A., interview with author.

33. Wexler, *Wounded Innocents*, 232.

34. L.A., interview with author.

35. Wexler, *Wounded Innocents*, 233.

36. Ibid.

37. Ibid., 235.

38. Faber, "The Real Abuse," 47.

Chapter Five

1. *Elements of a Model for Reform* (AZ: Arizona Civil Liberties Union, 1993), 3-4.

2. Ibid., 4.

3. Julie Szekely, "Pair Lost Custody of Girl Abused in Sitter's Home," *Tucson Citizen* (22 October 1993): 5D.

4. Julie Szekely, "One Family's 11-year-old Nightmare Not Over Yet," *Tucson Citizen* (22 October 1993): 5D.

5. Julie Szekely, "Tucsonians Complain about CPS," *Tucson Citizen* (21 October 1993): 8D.

6. Ibid.

7. Ibid.

8. Phoenix Memorial Hospital, "Child Sexual Abuse," *Arizona Republic* (19 July 1992): 10–1A.

9. *Corrupted Innocence* (CA: V.O.C.A.L., 1992), Video.

10. Ibid.

11. Ibid.

12. Ibid.

13. Julie Szekely, "Family's Fearful Separation Left Lasting Scars on the Children, Parents," *Tucson Citizen* (22 October 1993): 5D.

14. Jon R. Conte, *A Look at Child Sexual Abuse* (USA: National Committee for Prevention of Child Abuse, 1986), 13.

15. *Corrupted Innocence*.

16. W. Allan Gerneau, "School Prevention Programs Cannot Protect Children from Sexual Abuse," in *America's Children: Opposing Viewpoints*, ed. Carol Wekesser (San Diego: Greenhaven Press, 1991), 90.

17. Richard Wexler, *Wounded Innocents* (Buffalo, NY: Prometheus Books, 1990), 160.

18. Gerneau, "School Prevention Programs," 91.

19. Andrew Simons, "Parents Group Says System Fosters Abuse," *Up the Creek* (20 November 1987): 8.

20. Gerneau, "School Prevention Programs," 91.

21. Ibid, 92.

22. Ibid.

23. Ibid., 94.

24. *Corrupted Innocence.*

25. Lee Coleman, "Medical Examination for Sexual Abuse: Are We Being Told the Truth?, *Arizona V.O.C.A.L. Newsletter* (Sept/ Oct 1989): 3–4.

26. Karen Bailey, "Agencies Have Answers, Lack Funds to Solve Child Abuse Problems," *Rocky Mountain News* (30 October 1986): 45.

27. *Families in Crisis: Report No. 2* (San Diego, CA: San Diego Grand Jury, 1992), 26.

28. Ibid., 37.

29. Ibid., 38.

Chapter Six

1. K. L. Billingsley, "The Scientific War on Child Abuse," *National Review* (15 February 1993): 26.

2. Ibid.

3. Ibid.

4. Alison Young, "Sex-Therapy Devices, Photos Cast Firm in Critical Spotlight," *Arizona Republic* (20 September 1993): 2A.

5. Ibid., 1A.

6. Ibid., 2A.

7. Ibid.

8. Ibid.

9. Ibid.

10. Ibid.

11. Julie Szekely, "Report: CPS Violating Rights," *Tucson Citizen* (25 November 1992): 2A.

12. Mary Margaret Chapman, Letter to Mr. Rick Romley, *Arizona Republic* (29 May 1992).

13. Alison Young, "Therapy Made Boy Violent, Grandma Says," *Arizona Republic* (9 July 1992): 10A.

14. Ibid.

15. Chapman, letter.

16. Young, "Therapy Made Boy Violent, Grandma Says," 10A.

17. Alison Young, "Court: Hospital Wanted Boy Out of Sex Program," *Arizona Republic* (8 July 1992): 4A.

18. Phoenix Memorial Hospital, "Child Sexual Abuse," *Arizona Republic* (19 July 1992): 10-1A.

19. Ibid.

20. Ibid.

21. Mary Margaret Chapman, "Report on Ad Hoc Hearings," *V.O.C.A.L. Newsletter* (November/December 1992): 1.

22. Alison Young, "Sex Therapy 'Nightmare' or Cure?" *Arizona Republic* (26 July 1992): 7A.

23. Ibid., 8A.

24. Alison Young, "Sex Therapy Used on Kids Spurs Outcry," *Arizona Republic* (14 June 1992): 2A.

25. Ibid.

26. Alison Young, "Care Unit Disputes Sex Device," *Arizona Republic* (18 June 1992): 1B.

27. Alison Young, "Sex-Treatment is Called Child Abuse," *Arizona Republic* (14 June 1992): 12A.

28. Young, "Care Unit Disputes Sex Device," 1B.

29. Young, "Sex-Treatment is Called Child Abuse," 12A.

30. Alison Young, "State Senator Wages War on Sex Program," *Arizona Republic* (27 June 1992): 1A.

31. Young, "Sex-Treatment is Called Child Abuse," 12A.

32. Ibid.

33. Alison Young, "Ruling Due on Director of Sex-Offense Unit," *Arizona Republic* (1 August 1992): 1B.

34. Young, "Sex-Therapy Devices, Photos Cast Firm in Critical Spotlight," 2A.

35. Young, "Sex-Treatment is Called Child Abuse," 12A.

36. Alison Young, "Boys in Sex Therapy Shown Bondage Slides," *Arizona Republic* (24 June 1992): 6A.

37. Alison Young, "Hospital Defends Sex-Therapy Device," 4A.

38. Young, "Sex-Treatment is Called Child Abuse," 12A.

39. Alison Young, "Sex-Test Device Halted for Youth," *Arizona Republic* (24 June 1992): 9A.

40. Chapman, "Report on Ad Hoc Hearings," 2-3.

41. Alison Young, "Sex Therapy Debate Grows," *Arizona Republic* (2 August 1992): 2A.

42. Ibid.

Chapter Seven

1. *"Lost" in the System: The Problem in Context* (New York: Edna McConnell Foundation, 1992), 1.

2. *Families in Crisis: Report No. 2* (San Diego: San Diego Grand Jury, 1992), 24.

3. *"Lost" in the System: The Problem in Context,* 1.

4. *Corrupted Innocence* (CA: V.O.C.A.L., 1992), Video.

5. Joan Barthel, *For Children's Sake: The Promise of Family Preservation* (New York: Edna McConnell Foundation, 1992), 16.

6. Ibid., 17.

7. Ibid.

8. *Families in Crisis,* 29.

9. Ibid., 32.

10. Ibid., 29.

11. Ibid., 4.

12. Ibid., 36.

13. Ibid., 38.

14. Michael B. Mushlin, "Foster Care Cannot Protect Children from Child Abuse," in *America's Children: Opposing Viewpoints,* ed. Carol Wekesser (San Diego: Greenhaven Press, 1991), 103.

15. Richard Wexler, *Wounded Innocents* (Buffalo, NY: Prometheus

Books, 1990), 168.

16. Christine Kukka, "Slow Response to Foster Care Woes Draws Criticism," *Guy Gannet Services* (14 December 1988).

17. *Families in Crisis*, 24.

18. Karen Bailey, "Foster Care Supervision Found Inadequate," *Rocky Mountain News* (28 October 1986): 24.

19. Andrew Simmons, "Parents' Groups Says System Fosters Abuse," *Up the Creek* (20 November 1987): 9.

20. *Families in Crisis*, 25.

21. Ibid., 26.

22. Ibid., 25–6.

23. Tony Natale, "Abuse Group Files Complaint Against Home," *Tribune Newspapers* (8 April 1992): 1B.

24. Maria Lopez, "CPS Sued in Abuse Case," *Tucson Citizen* (23 December 1993): 1A.

25. Mushlin, "Foster Care Cannot Protect Children from Physical Abuse," 101.

26. Wexler, *Wounded Innocence*, 193.

27. Ibid., 199.

28. *Quick Facts About Family Preservation Services* (New York: Edna McConnell Foundation, 1992), 1.

Chapter Eight

1. Stephen J. Ceci and Maggie Bruck, "The Suggestibility of the Child Witness: A Historical Review and Synthesis of the Child Witness," *Psychological Review* (18 May 1992): 8.

2. Ibid., 25.

3. Ibid.

4. Ibid., 34.

5. Ibid., 51.

6. Ibid., 35.

7. Ibid., 4.

8. Ibid., 6.

9. Ibid., 31.

10. Ibid., 35-6.

11. Ibid., 36.

12. Ibid., 4.

13. "Figure This One Out," *Arizona V.O.C.A.L. Newsletter* (Nov/Dec 1992): 5.

14. Jane Hulse, "Dolls Play Role in Abuse Investigations," *Rocky Mountain News* (27 October 1986): 16.

15. Ceci and Brock, "The Suggestibility of the Child Witness," 37.

16. Ibid., 39.

17. Ibid., 37.

18. Ralph Underwager and Hollida Wakefield, "A Paradign Shift for Expert Witness," *Issues in Child Abuse Accusations*, vol. 5, no. 3 (1993): 161.

19. Ibid.

Chapter Nine

1. *Families in Crisis: Report No. 2* (San Diego: San Diego Grand Jury, 1992), 6.

2. Richard Wexler, *Wounded Innocents* (Buffalo, NY: Prometheus Books, 1990), 16.

3. Ibid., 15.

4. *Families in Crisis*, 26.

5. State of Washington, Department of Social and Health Services, Memorandum dated 16 March 1987.

6. Jane Hulse, "State's Blacklist Tracks Abuse Suspects," *Rocky Mountain News* (21 October 1986): 6.

7. Ibid.

8. Wexler, *Wounded Innocents*, 15.

9. Hulse, "State's Blacklist Tracks Abuse Suspects," 16.

10. Ibid.

11. Christopher J. Klicka, *The Right Choice: Homeschooling* (Oregon: Noble Publishing Associates, 1993), 122–3.

12. Ibid., 252.

13. Ibid., 256.

14. Ibid., 266–7.

15. *Families in Crisis*, 7.

16. Ibid., 8.

17. Ibid., 10–1.

18. Ibid., 10.

19. "Perverted Prosecution/Judges," *Arizona V.O.C.A.L. Newsletter* (January/February 1990): 4.

20. Klicka, *The Right Choice: Homeschooling*, 269.

21. Renee Ordway, "Old Town OKs Settlement for Harrington," *Bangor Daily News* (13–4 November 1993): 3.

22. *Families in Crisis*, 36–7.

23. Arthur Hagapian, "False Memories, Torn Families," *Sunday Eagle-Tribune* (28 March 1993): 2.

24. Ibid., 1.

25. Mark Kimble, "Child Protective Services Ruling Has Dad in Legal Limbo," *Tucson Citizen* (21 October 92): 17A.

26. Dee S. Knowles, Letter to the Editor, *Arizona V.O.C.A.L. Newsletter* (Sept/Oct 1991): 5.

27. Ibid.

Chapter Ten

1. Helen Dunahey, Letter to Captain Dave Reed Fremont County Sheriff (14 October 1992): entered as public record, case #93 CR 52-11.

2. P. D. Smith, Transcript of interview with Sheriff's Department (26 October 1992): Case #92-4807 (public record), 1.

3. Ibid., 2.

4. Motion to Disqualify the Honorable Julie G. Harshall, Fremont County District Court Case #93 CR 52-11 (27 December 1993): 2.

5. D. D. Heverly, sworn affidavit, Case #93 CR 52-11 (21 December 1993): 1.

6. Ibid.

7. J. E. Hernandez, sworn affidavit, Case #93 CR 52-11 (22 December 1993): 1.

8. P. E. Paris, sworn affidavit, Case #93 CR 52-11 (21 December 1993): 1.

9. B. Lancaster, sworn affidavit, Case #93 CR 52-11 (20 December 1993): 1.

10. V. Milligan, sworn affidavit, Case #93 CR 52-11 (22 December 1993): 1.

11. B. Lancaster, sworn affidavit, 2.

12. Motion to Disqualify, 2.

13. A.S. testimony from official transcript, Case #93, CR 52-11, 137.

14. Motion to Dismiss Charges, Case #93, CR 52-11 (11 February 1994): 1.

Chapter Eleven

1. Christopher J. Klicka, *The Right Choice: Homeschooling* (Grisham, OR: Noble Publishing Associates, 1993), 313.

2. Ibid., 55.

3. Ibid.

4. Ibid., 56.

5. Richard Wexler, *Wounded Innocents* (Buffalo, NY: Prometheus Books, 1990), 100.

6. Dr. James Hitchcock, "The Anti-Family Agenda," *Florida V.O.C.A.L. Newsletter*: 15.

7. James Garbarino, "Creating a Less Violent Society Can Protect Children from Physical Abuse," in *America's Children: Opposing Viewpoints* (San Diego: Greenhaven Press, 1991), 116.

8. Wexler, *Wounded Innocents*, 107.

9. Garbarino, "Creating a Less Violent Society," 103.

10. *Home Visitation for Primary Prevention of Child Abuse* (Englewood, CO: AHA, 1993), 1.

11. Vincent J. Fontana and Valerie Moolman, *Save the Family, Save the Child* (NY: Penquin Books USA, 1991), 173.

12. Ibid.

13. William F. Jasper, "Child Social Program and State Control," reprinted in *The Christian Report* (June/July 1992): 43.

14. Howard Cohen, *Equal Rights for Children* (Totawa, NJ: Rowen and Littlefield, 1980), 28.

15. Ibid.

Chapter Thirteen

1. "Revised Risk Factor Form" (MO: MO Department of Elementary and Secondary Education, PAT National Center, 1990).

2. Christopher J. Klicka, *The Right Choice: Homeschooling* (Oregon: Noble Publishing Associates, 1993), 258.